BEYOND NUMBERS, VALUES MATTER

Reimagining Business and Finance in a Data-Driven World

Opeyemi Aro

BEYOND NUMBERS, VALUES MATTER:

Reimagining Business and Finance in a Data-Driven
World

MCG

MCGILLIGAN PUBLISHING
3707 CYPRESS CREEK PKWY STE 310 #505
HOUSTON, TX 77068
www.mcgilliganpublishing.com

ISBN
Hardcover: 978-1-969844-39-3
Paperback: 978-1-969844-38-6

For those who strive to build a world where success is measured not just by profit, but by the impact we leave behind.

This book will inspire you to go beyond the numbers.

CONTENTS

INTRODUCTION

Consider this scenario: You are seated in a strategy meeting, listening to various presentations with data and metrics projected on the screen. All reports and proposals are filled with numbers, statistics, and charts that appear to justify the points being made. Yet, as everyone nods along, you have an uncomfortable feeling that something is missing.

So, you ask yourself, "Why doesn't all this data—despite being accurate and objective—seem to cover the whole picture?" But you're not sure how to voice your concerns. Maybe you're even feeling a slight sense of guilt. After all, as the well-trained professional that you are, are you not supposed to validate every opinion and decision with relevant data empirically?

Experts have told us that if we pay attention to the numbers, success is practically guaranteed. Yet, when we have to deal with real people and real situations on the basis of data alone, we find that the numbers don't always add up.

The harsh reality is that when data takes precedence over all other factors in decision-making, it can impair our judgment, putting ethical considerations and human values on the back burner.

Numbers are powerful, no doubt, but are they sufficient? How can we reconcile the quantitative focus of data-driven decision-making with the qualitative importance of human values?

As automation becomes increasingly prevalent, how do we ensure that business processes and decisions are guided by ethical values? What are we doing to instill a sense of moral responsibility in the next generation of business and finance leaders, especially as technology reshapes traditional work models?

While this book does not provide all the answers, it offers insights that can serve as guardrails to keep us grounded in the precarious days ahead.

If you have ever experienced that internal conflict between hitting your targets or fulfilling regulatory requirements without neglecting ethical considerations or violating your moral compass, you will find this book immensely useful. By the time you're done reading, you will have a framework for achieving sustainable success in your business or career while staying true to your values.

In the world of business and finance, data is often portrayed as an unbiased ally. But it is evident that numbers alone cannot adequately equip us to make decisions that are right, good, or fair. Actually, if we're being honest, we will admit that some of the biggest financial errors and business failures have been caused not by insufficient data but by an excessive dependence on it.

Data, no matter how detailed, can be like printing out black-and-white pictures from the scenes of a full-length movie produced in full color. Those pictures can give you some information about the movie, but they cannot tell the whole story.

Similarly, data might tell you what, but it can never tell you why. It lacks the wisdom that comes from values—values that keep us grounded, offer context, and clarify the things that truly matter.

There's no denying the critical place of data in business and finance. In fact, data is reshaping entire industries and creating new ones. But there's another side to that story. Although numbers offer precision, they cannot capture the nuances of ethical judgment, personal responsibility, and the broader consequences of our decisions.

In an age where automation and algorithms increasingly mediate or actually make decisions for us, it has become more important than ever to realize that beyond numbers, values matter.

For example, an automated system that evaluates candidates for promotion based solely on performance metrics may sound efficient. But have you factored in the possibility that these metrics could ignore soft skills and character traits like empathy or integrity?

Such a system might make financial sense in the short term, but in the long term, it will create a workplace culture that's hollow and, ultimately, unsustainable.

The finance industry is known to prioritize efficiency, objectivity, and profitability. These goals are certainly necessary. However, with the increasing emphasis on data, something even more important—human values—gets lost in the process. This imbalance is starkly illustrated by the stories of Enron, Lehman Brothers, Wells Fargo, and countless others.

When data and profit become the only indicators of success, the people behind the numbers often pay the price. And in many cases, the consequences are far-reaching, affecting others who are not even remotely involved.

How then do we balance the focus on numbers with the need for values? Is this even possible? The answer is a resounding yes! It's not only possible but also increasingly essential.

In this age of rapid advancement in technology, we must recognize that aligning our decisions with our values isn't just a "nice-to-have." It's a critical factor for building fulfilling careers and businesses that are not only resilient and sustainable but also trustworthy.

Please note that value-driven decision-making is not about disregarding data; rather, it's about using data as one tool among many. Numbers tell us what might work; values tell us what *should* work.

But what do we mean by values? And more importantly, how can we apply them without losing sight of our business goals and professional objectives?

Values are those guiding principles that define our sense of right and wrong, shaping the standards by which we make decisions.

Think of them as a moral compass. They're the difference between merely "getting ahead" and making a positive impact while at it. Now, values are not always easy to define. Unlike numbers, they're intangible and could even be invisible.

They're complex, shaped by personal experience, culture, and societal norms. And, to be fair, values can sometimes feel like an obstacle, especially in environments where you need to make fast, data-driven decisions to get ahead.

For example, imagine that as a business leader, you're considering a major cost-cutting move that will make your company more profitable but lead to a large reduction in the workforce. Data alone might say, "Go for it." But values urge you to ask, "At what cost?"

In a business landscape increasingly influenced by technology and automation, value-driven decision-making is often framed as idealistic. But in reality, values serve as a long-term strategy that drives both trust and loyalty—the foundations of any sustainable organization.

Companies like Patagonia, which famously prioritized environmental impact over rapid growth, have shown that sticking to values can foster not only customer loyalty but also industry respect. At first, it might look like a sacrifice, but value-driven decisions tend to pay off in ways that numbers alone could never predict.

This book is not about abandoning data. On the contrary, it's about empowering you to harness both data and values, creating a powerful synergy that guides better decisions.

It's about asking more from your analysis, going beyond the comfort of quantifiable outcomes to explore the deeper impact of your actions and decisions. In doing so, you'll find that numbers and values don't have to be in conflict. Instead, they can complement each other, creating a framework for decision-making that's both profitable and principled.

As you go through each chapter, you'll gain a fresh perspective on what it means to build a successful business and career—a perspective that combines quantitative insights with qualitative wisdom.

We will look at the history of traditional finance and explore how ethical considerations got relegated. We'll examine how personal values shape professional choices, and we'll challenge the limits of data as the sole foundation of strategy.

By the end, you'll be equipped not just with the "how" of value-driven decision-making but with the "why" that makes it all worthwhile.

So, if you've ever experienced a conflict between your professional goals and your personal values, or if you've ever wondered about the true cost of a data-driven decision, you're in good company. Let's take this journey together to find that sweet spot where numbers and values meet, reshaping the way you define success.

1

TRADITIONAL FINANCE AND VALUES

The finance unit of every organization has a clear purpose, doesn't it? Generate profit. Maximize cashflow. Increase shareholder value. For decades, traditional finance has been laser-focused on these goals. Strategies, models, and frameworks—nearly all cornerstones of finance— have been constructed with one purpose in mind: to maximize returns. It's a system built on precision and efficiency, supported by an almost mathematical logic.

But despite the profits and prestige, many professionals and business leaders have started to wonder if something is missing.

With each financial decision aimed at creating value on a balance sheet, a quiet question lingers in the background: Where do values fit in?

Understand that by values, we're not talking about numbers or valuations but human principles, ethics, integrity, and fairness. Can a system designed to maximize numbers also support human-centric values? It's a question more people in the industry are beginning to ask.

You may be thinking that the system has worked well enough without values taking the front seat. After all, traditional finance has been a cornerstone of global economic growth, enabling cross-border investment, fostering innovation, and building the foundations for today's interconnected markets.

Yet, high-profile scandals and collapses such as Enron, Lehman Brothers, or the 2008 financial crisis seem to signal an imbalance, a crack in the system.

Each of these events, driven by unchecked ambition, complex financial instruments, and aggressive risk-taking, caused massive societal repercussions. Could the absence of values be the underlying cause? It's a possibility we can't ignore.

Profit vs. Principle: The Core Dilemma

At its core, traditional finance is positioned as the ultimate problem solver. It is needed for everything you want to establish, and you are most likely to resort to it because it has been a convention. Let's understand that through examples. Do you need to build a hospital? Issue a bond. Are you launching a new tech startup? Seek angel investors.

But here's the paradox: while finance funds progress, they can also compromise ethics in the name of profit.

Finance professionals are often trained to look at numbers without questioning the ethical implications behind them. That's how terms like "externalities," "encumbrance," and "moral hazard" became part of the finance lexicon—concepts that allow the system to consider profits over principles, often to the detriment of the larger society.

Imagine, for example, a hedge fund manager eyeing a new investment opportunity: a company showing impressive profits but with a record of polluting the environment.

Traditional finance might say, "If it's profitable, invest!" However, what it fails to take into consideration is the possibility of an adversity that is bound to happen. Factors such as what happens to the environment or society if this pattern repeats across thousands of investment decisions are more often than not ignored entirely.

This "profit over principle" mindset can create a cascading impact that no financial model can measure.

The truth is that traditional finance has set up a system that sometimes ignores the consequences of its actions. When profit is the primary objective, principles can be regarded as costly, inconvenient detours.

And while profit-focused decision-making can lead to short-term gains, it often comes at a cost. This cost might not appear on the balance sheet, but it surfaces elsewhere in the social and environmental fabric of our lives.

A Lesson on Prioritizing Principle Over Profit

A marketing manager for a consumer goods company found herself at odds with her team during the launch of a new product. The product was aimed at young children, and her team proposed a series of advertisements designed to appeal emotionally to parents.

However, during a review of the campaign materials, she noticed that the ads made exaggerated claims about the product's benefits—claims that were not fully supported by research data.

When she raised her concerns, the response from her team was dismissive. They argued that the ads would perform exceptionally well and boost early sales, which were crucial to recouping the high costs of product development.

Still, she held firm, believing that misleading customers, especially when the target audience included children, was unethical.

She escalated the matter to the senior management and proposed reworking the campaign to emphasize the product's proven benefits rather than inflated claims. Though this delayed the launch and led to initial tensions, the revised campaign performed well and was widely praised for its authenticity. Her decision safeguarded the company's reputation and reinforced its commitment to ethical marketing practices.

Like the marketing manager in this story, business leaders and professionals should never forget that integrity is the cornerstone of lasting success. Resist the pressure to overpromise or mislead, even if it seems beneficial in the short term. Honesty in communication strengthens trust with customers and safeguards a company's reputation.

The Cultural Roots of Profit-Driven Finance

Why does traditional finance prioritize profit so heavily? Part of the answer lies in its history. In many ways, modern finance was born out of industrialization.

The 18th and 19th centuries saw a wave of innovation and productivity, with finance playing a central role. Back then, growth and capital accumulation were the keys to survival in a rapidly industrializing world. Finance's role was clear-cut: it was there to accelerate economic growth.

Over time, this profit-driven focus became embedded in the culture of finance. The heroes of

Wall Street and financial success stories around the world celebrated profits, power, and growth above all. This culture of prioritizing profits over principles has persisted, reinforced by incentives, rewards, recognition, and the societal prestige that comes with financial success.

In the process, values like integrity, fairness, and responsibility have been relegated. They are generally seen as admirable but not essential to success.

This cultural foundation shapes the way finance professionals are trained. Finance education often focuses on models, metrics, and efficiency. Risk is measured, but the "human" cost is often overlooked. When we talk about a "solid investment," we mean one that yields high returns, not one that necessarily supports society.

Consequently, traditional finance has built a culture where numbers reign supreme and values, or ethical considerations can feel like afterthoughts.

The Influence of Metrics and Data

If finance had a language, it would be data. Numbers, ratios, and percentages drive decisions, and there's a sense of comfort in that. Numbers feel objective, dependable, and free from bias. But let's face it: do numbers always tell the full story? Not really.

Data in finance is powerful, yet it has limits. While metrics like ROI (Return on Investment) and EPS (Earnings Per Share) reveal profitability, they don't account for the broader impact on the workforce, communities, or the environment.

Data can tell you if a company's stock is performing well, but it may not necessarily show if that company is mistreating its workers or damaging the environment. In this way, data creates a narrow view that leaves values out of the equation.

Consider the rise of algorithms in trading. Today, financial algorithms execute trades at speeds and scales that humans can't match. But these algorithms don't "see" the human or environmental impact of their trades. What they mainly focus on is profit. It is the only thing that they "see."

In an industry increasingly driven by metrics, this approach can create a gap between finance and its broader social responsibilities. When the only objective is to "beat the market," the human cost becomes invisible.

The Hidden Costs of Ignoring Values

Numbers can make finance feel precise, almost scientific. But, ironically, the pursuit of profit without values introduces unpredictability. When financial decisions are made without considering their broader impacts, it creates a ripple effect, leading to consequences that numbers alone can't predict.

When business and finance leaders ignore values, they are essentially building an edifice on a shaky foundation; eventually, the structure will fail.

Take the 2008 financial crisis as a prime example. Driven by a hunger for higher returns, financial institutions engaged in high-risk lending and complex derivatives trading. The immediate returns were impressive, but these strategies ultimately proved unsustainable.

When the market crashed, the impact was global, resulting in lost jobs, home foreclosures, and a recession that affected millions. What can we learn from this? When values are left out of financial decisions, the consequences can reach beyond the boardroom.

The hidden costs of ignoring values are
often borne by society at large.

Short-term profits may come at the expense of long-term trust, environmental health, or social stability. And in a world where information is more readily accessible than ever, the reputational risk is also significant.

This is not only true for organizations but also for individuals. We will have a saner world when the vast majority of business leaders and corporate professionals are driven not just by profit and rewards but by values and principles.

Values as a Competitive Advantage

It may sound counterintuitive, but values can be a competitive advantage in business and finance. It is to be understood that trust is something that does not come easily. It is earned, and while it is earned, it also enjoys the reputation of being a rare commodity. In a world where trust is eroded by scandals and missteps, a company, institution, or individual that prioritizes ethical principles can easily stand out.

Trustworthiness builds client loyalty and
fosters long-term partnerships.

Think about companies like BlackRock, which launched environmental, social, and governance (ESG) funds in response to growing demand for ethical investments. By aligning with values that matter to investors, they've attracted billions of dollars in assets. It turns out that people want to invest in companies that reflect their own principles. Consequently, a value-driven approach doesn't just foster goodwill—it also meets market demand.

Embracing value-driven finance might
seem like going out on a limb, but in practice,
it's a path to long-term sustainability and
resilience.

Companies that incorporate values into their decision-making processes are better equipped to weather crises, as they're often less exposed to reputation-damaging risks. In an industry built on trust, these values can help companies build a solid, lasting foundation. After all, when clients trust you, they're more likely to stay loyal, even when market downturns.

Reimagining Finance with Values at the Core

So, where does this leave us? Traditional finance has followed a straightforward path, with profit as its primary compass. But as we've seen, this single-minded pursuit can be limiting, even damaging. It's time to reimagine what finance can be.

Let us adopt a new paradigm where values and profit coexist—not in opposition but in harmony.

To make this shift, business leaders and professionals need a broader framework that includes not only financial returns but also ethical returns.

This reimagined approach to finance requires a commitment to responsibility and accountability. It requires the willingness of business leaders to look beyond short-term gains and ask the hard questions: What impact will this decision have? Who benefits, and who might bear the cost?

Imagine a finance system that prioritizes ethical investment and encourages companies to balance profit with purpose. Such a system isn't just good for society, but it's also good for business.

Companies with strong ethical practices generally outperform their peers over the long term. In other words, values don't detract from profit; they enhance it.

The finance industry can drive social good, support sustainable growth, and empower communities. When values are embraced as part of the core mission, finance can be a force for positive change.

Bringing Values into Focus

In this chapter, we have identified a major issue in traditional finance—the tension between profit and principle. It's an issue that won't disappear overnight. But by acknowledging it, we can start to rethink performance standards and redefine success in a way that is both profitable and sustainable.

As you move forward in this book, you'll discover practical ways to bring values into your decision-making. This is not just about compliance or looking good. It's about integrating values into every detail of your life and work, from daily transactions to major investments, because you have realized that beyond numbers, values matter.

2

WHY NUMBERS ALONE ARE NOT ENOUGH

We've all been there—sitting in meetings or poring over reports, where the conversation seems entirely dominated by numbers. It feels like everything that matters has been reduced to metrics, KPIs, profit margins, and growth rates. The fact is, numbers can make complex realities feel manageable and neatly packaged, reducing uncertainty and ambiguity in an increasingly volatile world. In finance, data is king—it drives decisions, shapes strategies, and offers insights that, ideally, reduce risk.

This conventional, data-driven approach to finance has produced remarkable precision, empowering individuals and organizations to make informed predictions, manage risk with greater accuracy, and progressively optimize performance. With the click of a button, you can access a world of metrics, algorithms, and predictive models, all working to provide answers grounded in numbers.

But behind every number, there's a choice about what to measure and how to interpret it. While data can indeed offer precision, it doesn't always tell the full story.

Numbers can be revealing, but they can also be misleading, especially if we assume that all necessary truths are captured in a dataset.

When business leaders and finance professionals rely exclusively on data, critical elements—like ethics, human impact, and social consequences— often get left behind.

In this chapter, we will take a closer look at the benefits and limitations of a purely data-driven approach and consider how we might balance data with the values that matter.

The Power of Data: Precision, Predictability, and Performance

There's no denying the power data brings to the world of business and finance. It allows for precision that was unimaginable even a few decades ago. Whether it's determining creditworthiness, analyzing market trends, or measuring return on investment (ROI), data gives professionals the ability to make informed decisions. It's the backbone of modern finance—a tool that enables financial institutions to predict trends, model risk, and maximize returns.

Think about algorithms that analyze thousands of stocks in seconds, providing portfolio managers with recommendations that minimize risk and maximize returns. Data-driven insights allow these managers to make better decisions faster, often with remarkable accuracy.

For example, algorithmic trading—a strategy where computers execute trades at speeds humans can't match—relies on data to spot price patterns and execute orders. This level of precision would be impossible without data.

But the benefits don't stop there. Data-driven decision-making has democratized access to financial markets. Retail investors can access financial tools, analytics, and insights previously available only to large institutions. This has allowed more people to participate in the financial ecosystem, expanding opportunities and increasing financial literacy.

The Limitations of Data: Blindness to Ethical Implications and Long-term Impact

In spite of all its power, data has significant limitations. It's a double-edged sword that brings precision but leaves out the nuances that guide our decisions. As a result of this, data only gives us a partial view of reality. When we are solely focused on factors that can be measured, critical but intangible factors—such as ethical implications or long-term impact—are often disregarded. This creates a gap between what the data shows and what truly matters.

For example, let's consider an investment model that relies solely on profit projections. The company involved might be underpaying its workers or producing high levels of waste.

While the model might accurately predict profit, it fails to capture the human and environmental costs. And what's the outcome? A shortsighted decision that appears profitable in theory but is actually detrimental to the larger ecosystem.

This shows that when we make decisions on the basis of numbers alone, we are likely to ignore the bigger picture—potentially causing harm to people, communities, and the environment.

Data, for all its accuracy, doesn't always provide context, and context is crucial to understanding the full impact of business and financial decisions.

Furthermore, an over-reliance on numbers can make companies more vulnerable. For example, many startups focus heavily on user growth metrics as a measure of success. Rapid growth looks impressive to investors and suggests a promising future. But if that growth isn't accompanied by a sustainable business model or a solid foundation of customer satisfaction, the company risks collapsing under its own weight.

Numbers alone can't capture the resilience and adaptability needed for long-term success.

They give us important data points, but they're not substitutes for a sustainable business strategy.

When companies ignore values and prioritize short-term metrics like quarterly revenue targets or cost-cutting, they may inadvertently encourage practices that erode customer trust and employee well-being.

These ignored values don't always have immediate financial consequences, but they affect the company's long-term health. Values also play a critical role in innovation. When a company's culture encourages ethical decision-making and prioritizes integrity, employees feel empowered to propose ideas that may challenge the status quo.

They're less likely to pursue shortcuts that could lead to ethical breaches or reputational damage and more likely to develop solutions that align with the company's mission. In this way, values provide a moral compass that keeps companies on course as they navigate the uncertainties of a rapidly changing market.

The Myth of Objectivity in Data

For as long as most of us can remember, business wisdom has told us that the numbers don't lie. Experts would have us believe that numbers are impartial and free from human biases. But that's not entirely true. Data is not as neutral as it appears. The process of gathering, analyzing, and interpreting data involves human choices every step of the way—choices about what to measure, how to measure it, and what conclusions to draw. These decisions introduce subjectivity, creating biases that can skew results, sometimes in fundamentally dubious ways.

Think about credit scoring, a widely used data-driven tool in finance. While credit scores are based on objective data points—payment history, debt levels, length of credit history—they can also reinforce social inequalities. If an individual has limited access to credit as a result of socioeconomic factors, their score may unfairly reflect a higher risk. In this way, a system intended to be fair and objective can, in practice, perpetuate bias.

This myth of objectivity is especially problematic because it can lead to overconfidence in data-driven decisions. When we believe data is infallible, we're less likely to question the ethical implications of decisions based on it. This can create a blind spot that allows harmful practices to go unchecked because they're "just following the data."

The Danger of "Justifying" Harmful Practices with Data

Business and finance leaders sometimes hide behind data-driven decisions to justify actions that are otherwise ethically questionable.

When a decision is supported by "the numbers," it can feel easier to suppress conscience and overlook potential consequences.

This is even more likely when those consequences impact individuals or groups who are not directly involved in the decision-making process.

Consider a scenario where a company decides to cut costs by outsourcing jobs to regions with lower labor costs. On paper, this decision reduces expenses and boosts profits, leading to a positive outcome for shareholders. However, the human impact—job losses, wage cuts, and economic downturns in affected communities—doesn't show up in the immediate financial data.

In this way, data-driven decisions can be used as a shield to justify practices that prioritize numbers over people. Ultimately, such decisions can have a negative impact on the company's reputation and erode trust with stakeholders.

To rely solely on data is to strip out the
human element, reducing people to variables
in a model and risks in a portfolio.

When that happens, we lose sight of the many significant ways in which our decisions affect society, the environment, and individual lives.

Protecting Employee Welfare Over Metrics

A branch manager in a regional banking institution shared a moment that tested her commitment to her team's well-being.

The bank had introduced a new target-based performance incentive to drive higher sales of financial products. A junior customer service officer approached her, visibly distressed.

The officer revealed that a top-ranking client, enticed by a high-value investment plan, had been making inappropriate remarks and creating an uncomfortable working environment.

When the situation was reported to higher management, the response was lukewarm. The directive was clear: the deal was too lucrative to lose, and the officer should find a way to "manage" the situation.

However, the branch manager couldn't accept this. Despite knowing it could negatively impact the branch's numbers, she immediately took steps to shield the officer by reassigning them and confronting the client directly. She explained that the bank valued ethical conduct and would not tolerate such behavior, even at the cost of losing the deal.

While the branch faced temporary financial pressure, her actions sent a strong message about the company's values. Over time, her stance fostered a culture where team members felt supported and empowered to prioritize personal dignity over performance pressures.

This story reinforces the fact that prioritizing people over numbers fosters loyalty and builds a workplace culture grounded in respect and ethics. Professionals are expected to be empathetic leaders who balance performance with dignity and fairness.

The Hidden Cost of Ignoring Values

Ignoring intangible factors—such as employee well-being, community impact, or ethical alignment—can come with a high cost. Companies that neglect these factors often face backlash, whether in the form of consumer boycotts, employee turnover, or regulatory scrutiny. Consequently, an approach that ignores values in favor of data alone can actually portend greater risk in the long run.

Take the example of the environmental impact of fossil fuels. For years, oil and gas companies relied on data that showed strong profits from fossil fuel extraction. But as awareness of climate change grew, so did public and regulatory pressure on these companies to consider the environmental cost of their operations.

Today, many of these firms are being held accountable, not only by governments but also by investors and consumers who want sustainable energy sources.

When you prioritize numbers over values, you might miss critical opportunities to build trust, foster loyalty, and drive sustainable growth.

These are benefits that may not always appear in a performance appraisal or quarterly report, but they are intangible assets that will deliver a tangible return on investment over time.

Balancing Precision with Principles

So, where does that leave us? Data is indispensable to finance, but it shouldn't be the only guide. For a system that impacts billions of lives, it's essential to balance precision with principles. That means rethinking data's role—not as the ultimate decisive factor but as one piece of the puzzle. One of the ways to achieve this balance is by implementing "values-based" metrics, which assess not only financial performance but also ethical alignment.

Imagine a framework where financial models include "social impact scores" alongside traditional metrics like ROI. By incorporating such metrics, business leaders and finance professionals can make more holistic decisions that align business goals with the greater good.

Another approach is the adoption of Environmental, Social, and Governance (ESG) metrics. ESG data provides investors with insights into a company's environmental and social impact, as well as its governance practices.

This kind of information goes beyond financial performance, giving investors a fuller picture of a company's values and its long-term sustainability. It's a shift toward a data-driven approach that respects values—a move away from raw numbers and toward a more nuanced understanding of what makes a company worth investing in.

Bringing the Human Element into the Equation

In the end, finance is about people. Every number in a data set represents something real: a worker's job, a family's livelihood, or a community's well-being. When business and finance leaders remember this, they can bring humanity back into the equation, finding a middle ground where data and values intersect.

As discussed earlier, this human-centered perspective is not about ignoring data or abandoning quantitative methods. It's about broadening the scope of what data means in finance, which also keeps ethics in the loop. It's also about moving beyond numbers and seeing the people and values behind them.

By bringing the human element back into finance, we will be better positioned to make more ethical decisions while also building a finance system that is resilient, inclusive, and trusted by society.

Embracing a Balanced Approach

Data remains essential to informed decision-making. But as we've seen, data alone isn't enough to address the complexities of the real world. A balanced approach—one that combines data with values—can create a finance system that is both precise and principled.

As we continue through this book, we'll explore strategies for balancing data with ethics in practical, actionable ways. We'll look at tools and frameworks that can help bring values into data-driven decision-making.

Remember, the point is not about choosing between data and values; it's about learning how to integrate the two for decisions that are both smart and ethical.

Let's redefine the role of data in finance, not as a barrier to values but as a bridge to more informed, compassionate, and sustainable decision-making.

3

VALUE-DRIVEN DECISION-MAKING FRAMEWORK

The process of decision-making, particularly in finance, is often predominantly established on calculations and strategic analysis. But value-driven decision-making requires us to look beyond the formulas and projections.

It's about connecting each choice to the values that represent our purpose, commitment, and vision. So, what does it mean to make decisions that are truly "value-driven," and why does this approach matter now more than ever?

In a fast-paced, data-focused world, companies face immense pressure to show tangible results. Metrics drive nearly every move, from forecasting earnings to assessing new projects. But in our pursuit of precision, it's easy to lose sight of the "why" behind those numbers without even realizing it.

Making decisions guided by values shows that success isn't only about reaching goals, it's about making sure you're aiming for the right ones in the first place.

In this chapter, we'll break down the essential elements of value-driven decision-making. We will discuss why it has its significance and review a framework that can guide us.

Prioritizing the Things That Matter Most

Making value-driven decisions requires a shift in mindset. Beyond asking, "What will bring the highest ROI?" you also ask, "What aligns with our core purpose and long-term mission?"

Let's say your company is committed to sustainability, and you are presented with an opportunity to partner with a supplier offering a lower cost but a poor environmental record. From a purely financial perspective, the partnership could boost profits and increase market competitiveness.

But with a value-driven framework, the question shifts.

The decision becomes less about cost-cutting and more about whether this partnership aligns with the company's values and its commitment to sustainability. More so, there are a lot of risks that come with such a partnership. So, organizations must also ask the question of whether it is even worth giving it a shot because it cuts costs but comes with consequences and damages that may not even be reversible.

It's a choice to prioritize principles over short-term gains, a step toward authentic value-driven decision-making.

To adopt this approach, you need to be intentional about identifying what matters most. In a world where practically everyone claims to prioritize "integrity" or "responsibility," true value-driven decision-making compels you to go beyond words and make deliberate choices that align your actions with your stated purpose.

As you consistently act in ways that reinforce the things that matter most, you will make decisions that cultivate not only financial success but also a meaningful legacy. Let's consider the case of Dangote, who bet on Africa when the odds were against him.

Aliko Dangote's story is about conviction, not wealth. At a time when the world was pouring money into Big Tech, Dangote had the chance to join that wave. If he had, his fortune today could easily have eclipsed $120 billion. Yet he turned his back on Silicon Valley's opportunities to mint billions and chose instead to confront Africa's hardest problems.

He put his money into cement, sugar, salt, and, later one of the world's largest oil refineries. These are areas most investors ran away from because they were heavy, risky, and plagued by infrastructure and policy hurdles, especially in Africa. Dangote knew the odds were stacked against him. But he also knew this: Africa could never truly rise without solving its foundational gaps. Cement to build. Sugar and salt to feed. Refineries to power growth.

This was not a safe bet. It was a sacrifice outweighing a financial fork in the road. A true defining moment. He could have stayed comfortable importing goods and cashing in margins. Instead, he tied his fortune to Africa's industrial future. Every factory he built, every job he created, every ton of cement that replaced imports was a statement: Africa must build for itself, and the world must respect it.

Today, Dangote stands as one of the wealthiest people alive, not because he chased the fastest trend, but because he held on to a deeper value: wealth is only meaningful when it transforms lives and industries.

For entrepreneurs, his story delivers a timeless truth. Real vision is not chasing the next big thing; it is building the thing your people cannot live without. The riskiest move is often the most rewarding when it is anchored in purpose. Legacy outlasts valuation.

Dangote is not just Nigeria's story. He is Africa's story to the world. He built industries. He proved that Africa could produce what it consumed, and in doing so, shifted the narrative from dependence to self-reliance.

A Framework for Value-Driven Decision-Making

Value-driven decision-making is not a vague aspiration; it's a concrete approach that can be structured and implemented through a clearly defined framework. Let's break down the key components of this framework.

1. Clarity of Values

Before any value-driven decision can take place, there must be clarity around your values, whether as an individual or as an organization. Organizations often display values like "innovation," "transparency," and "diversity" on their websites and in annual reports, but these values actually have no meaning because they do not reflect in day-to-day operations.

Clarity of values involves translating these ideals into actionable guidelines that inform every choice, large or small.

For instance, if a company values "employee well-being," it must define how that translates into decisions about work hours, health benefits, or even layoff strategies.

How often does the company carry out pulse surveys to gauge employees' current feelings about their work environment, workloads, and overall satisfaction? How often are engagement surveys administered to assess how connected employees feel to their work, team, and company? Have you ever wondered why some initiatives or new business projects fail due to these blind spots?

Values must be more than words—they should serve as a compass that guides decisions across all departments. It is, therefore, absolutely important that these values are communicated and understood, not just by leadership but throughout the organization.

2. Stakeholder Consideration

Companies that focus solely on numbers usually base their decisions on whatever works best for shareholders. On the other hand, companies that adopt a value-driven approach take into account the unique perspectives and expectations of a broad set of stakeholders.

They consider how their decisions will affect shareholders, customers, employees, suppliers, and communities. This focus on interested parties helps companies avoid isolated decision-making that only prioritizes immediate, profit-driven outcomes.

For example, imagine that your company is faced with a major operational decision, such as relocating to a cheaper region. From a financial standpoint, the move might be a no-brainer.

But a value-driven decision-making framework will make you consider the impact on local employees, the community you're leaving behind, and the community you're moving into.

Balancing financial benefits with stakeholder interests can foster loyalty, trust, and goodwill.

These are essential factors that can be difficult to quantify but are crucial if you want to succeed over the long term.

3. Long-Term Orientation

Business leaders and finance professionals are often tempted to focus on short-term gains, but a value-driven approach emphasizes sustainability and long-term impact. To adopt a long-term orientation is to resist the pressure for immediate results in favor of choices that will sustain your mission over time. This doesn't mean ignoring short-term success. It simply means balancing short-term needs with a strategic, long-term perspective.

An example here is product development. Some companies might rush a product to market to beat competitors, even if it's not fully refined. A value-driven framework encourages asking, "Is this choice consistent with our commitment to quality and customer satisfaction?" By focusing on long-term outcomes, you avoid compromising on values for the sake of expediency.

4. Ethical Consistency

In value-driven decision-making, ethical considerations are not an afterthought; they're foundational.

Ethical consistency means holding every decision to the same ethical standards, regardless of potential financial gain.

This approach challenges you to consider the moral implications of your actions. It also ensures that they are consistent with both internal values and external social responsibilities or legal requirements.

Take, for example, a decision about data privacy. For many companies, data collection is a valuable tool for understanding customer behavior and improving products. However, a value-driven company will assess the ethical implications of collecting and using personal data, ensuring that privacy standards are met and that customer trust is prioritized over purely economic benefits. In this way, ethical consistency fosters integrity while also helping to maintain public trust.

5. Measuring Impact Beyond Financials

Finally, value-driven decision-making includes assessing outcomes beyond profit margins. Financial metrics remain essential, but they're complemented by impact metrics that reflect the organization's values. These can include employee well-being, customer satisfaction, environmental sustainability, and community impact.

For instance, a company could measure its success not only by quarterly revenue but also by its carbon footprint reduction, employee engagement scores, or community contributions. This approach recognizes that profit is only one aspect of a company's overall bearing, and that real success is multidimensional.

Implementing the Framework for Value-Driven Decisions

In most cases, implementing value-driven decision-making requires a change in both mindset and practice. Here are some practical steps you can take to begin putting this framework into action, whether as an individual or as an organization:

1. Define and Document Core Values

Start by clearly defining your core values in a way that goes beyond general statements. Each value should include specific, actionable examples to provide clarity and direction. For instance, if "environmental responsibility" is a core value, document the specific practices that support this, like reducing energy use or sourcing from sustainable suppliers.

2. Create Decision-Making Guidelines

Develop strategies that map out how values should influence decision-making. This can take the form of a decision matrix or checklist that includes values as key criteria. When making a significant choice, you can use this matrix to ensure that each option aligns with your core principles.

3. Engage Stakeholders in the Process

Include participation from a diverse group of stakeholders, especially those that will be affected by your decisions. This helps ensure that the impact on customers, employees, and communities is considered at every stage. Regularly consulting stakeholders builds trust, which in turn creates an environment where everyone's voice is valued.

4. Develop Impact Metrics

Go beyond traditional financial metrics to measure the outcomes of value-driven decisions. For example, an organization can develop specific metrics for areas such as employee satisfaction, environmental impact, and social contribution. These additional metrics provide a more comprehensive view of the organization's progress, showing not just profitability but a positive impact.

5. Commit to Accountability and Transparency

Finally, accountability and transparency are essential for maintaining a value-driven approach. Communicate openly about the decision-making process, especially in cases where there's a conflict between financial and ethical considerations. Transparency builds trust and portrays your commitment to acting in alignment with your values, even when it's challenging.

Challenges and Misconceptions of Value-Driven Decision-Making

Implementing value-driven decision-making is not always easy; it comes with its challenges. One common misconception is that value-driven decisions are inherently unprofitable or impractical. This belief stems from a short-term view focused on immediate results. But as we've discussed, value-driven decisions often yield benefits that enhance long-term profitability and resilience.

Another challenge is balancing conflicting values. Sometimes, two core values may appear to be in opposition. For example, profitability and environmental responsibility. In these cases, the decision becomes a matter of prioritization, weighing options carefully to find a middle ground that honors your values as fully as possible.

Furthermore, people sometimes confuse value-driven decision-making with following gut feelings, but it is much deeper than that. It's about consciously choosing an appropriate course of action based on predetermined and clearly defined principles. We will explore the connection between values and gut feelings in another chapter.

Lastly, value-driven decision-making requires courage. Choosing the value-driven path often involves taking a stand, potentially going against market trends, defying popular logic, and resisting the pressure for quick gains.

It may be easier to prioritize the bottom line, but the professionals and organizations that embrace values will stand out.

They will develop the kind of resilience needed to achieve long-term success instead of just being a flash in the pan.

A New Lens for Decision-Making

Value-driven decision-making isn't just a framework, it's a mindset, a lens through which we view every choice, big or small. As we learn to instill values into our decision-making processes, we lay the foundation for a culture that balances profit with purpose. In a world where more stakeholders are beginning to demand transparency and responsibility, this balanced approach is not just desirable. It's essential.

4

Values in High-Stakes Environments

In a world that demands speed and precision, values can sometimes seem like luxuries—nice to have but easily lost in the heat of the moment. Yet, it's in these very moments of pressure that our values need to come to the surface, serving as a reliable compass to guide us through the complexities of a situation.

Value-driven decision-making becomes even more challenging when the stakes are high and pressure is mounting.

Making clear, ethical decisions in such situations can feel like driving through fog. In this chapter, we will continue our discussion on creating a framework for value-driven decision-making with specific application to high-stakes situations.

Understanding the Psychological and Emotional Impact of High-Stakes Situations

Let's be honest—high-stakes environments change how we think, feel, and react. Imagine a situation where a key project deadline is at risk, with reputations, jobs, or company goals on the line. The tension in such moments isn't just mental; it's physical, too.

Your heart races, palms get sweaty, and time feels like it's slipping away faster than you can act. Underneath it all, the mind slips into "fight or flight," increasing the pressure to resolve things quickly, almost at any cost.

In these moments, there's a natural shift in priorities. Logic and values sometimes take a backseat, while survival instincts take over.

The need to protect, to win, to defend—all of these can cloud judgment, even for the most seasoned professionals. Have you ever noticed how people under pressure might lean into "quick fixes" that don't entirely sit right?

Maybe a manager fudges a report to meet a looming deadline or an employee cuts corners to avoid potential backlash. These actions often don't stem from a lack of understanding of integrity or other values; they stem from a lack of time to think.

It's crucial to understand how pressure impacts us in order to recognize ethical dilemmas in these situations. High-stakes environments can create a tunnel vision where the brain selectively focuses on immediate solutions. This often leads the brain to shut out long-term considerations. This is exactly why ethical conflicts can slip by unnoticed. The more aware we are of this natural tendency, the better we can guard against it.

Identifying Common Ethical Conflicts in Fast-Paced Environments

Ethical dilemmas in fast-paced settings do not announce themselves with a warning label. Instead, they blend into the rush, often disguised as standard decisions or routine choices. But ethical conflicts do have patterns, and when you know what to look for, you will be better equipped to spot them.

One common dilemma revolves around transparency versus performance. Imagine a sales team that's been struggling to hit its targets all quarter, with performance reviews around the corner. The temptation to inflate numbers "just this once" can feel harmless, especially if everyone's feeling the pressure.

But ask yourself, "What am I willing to compromise for short-term gains?" This is a powerful diagnostic question that quietly tests your integrity.

Another classic scenario could appear in the form of resource allocation. Let's say you're managing a project with a limited budget and an even tighter timeline. It can be tempting to cut costs by using cheaper materials, even if it slightly impacts the quality. Before you know it, it becomes a norm for you to use materials that are cheap and allow you to cut costs, even if it means having an impact on the quality produced, no matter how minimal that impact might be.

The underlying question in this case isn't always clear: is the slight dip in quality acceptable to meet your deadline, or is it compromising on a promise made to stakeholders?

These subtle dilemmas often lurk beneath the surface, masked by the daily grind and urgency.

Learning to recognize them means paying close attention to the tiny nudges we feel when something feels "off." It's about listening to that quiet internal voice questioning, "Is this really right?" rather than simply asking, "Is this doable?"

Practical Illustration: Choosing Sustainability Over Cost-Cutting

A procurement officer at a manufacturing company shared an experience where he had to make a values-based decision regarding suppliers. The company was under significant financial pressure and looking to cut costs across all departments. His manager tasked him with finding a cheaper supplier for raw materials, emphasizing the need to slash expenses quickly.

During his research, he discovered that the most affordable supplier had a poor record of environmental violations and exploited labor in their operations. Although switching to this supplier would significantly reduce costs, he believed that it went against the company's stated commitment to sustainability and ethical business practices.

He took a bold step by presenting alternative suppliers who aligned with the company's values, even though they were slightly more expensive. While this decision delayed the cost-cutting initiative, it reinforced the company's integrity and later earned them recognition from industry stakeholders for their sustainable practices. Also, the damages were reduced to zero when they could have been a lot had the manager gone with the supplier who sold the raw material at prices that best suited the cost-cutting initiative.

The procurement officer's story highlights the courage it takes to align decisions with broader values, even under intense financial constraints.

Individuals and organizations that choose to align decisions with ethical and sustainable practices demonstrate long-term vision and accountability. They understand that short-term savings can never outweigh the long-term costs of compromising values.

Warning Signals to Watch Out For

The tricky part of ethical compromises is that they're often gradual. Rarely does someone set out to disregard their values overnight. Rather, it's a slow erosion, one small decision at a time. So, what are the signs that values might be slipping?

1. Fake Sense of Justification

First, there's a sense of justification creeping into decisions. Phrases like "It's just this once," or "Everybody does it," are warning signals. They reveal a shift from absolute principles to relative convenience. If you or your team find yourselves rationalizing questionable choices, it's often a sign that the decision is skirting ethical boundaries.

2. A Constant Reminder

Another red flag is the feeling of discomfort or guilt that follows a choice. This can look like a nagging thought that replays in your mind or a subtle feeling of unease that lingers after a decision. When we're aligned with our values, decisions feel clean and clear. When something's off, our conscience tends to remind us, even if quietly. The challenge is to listen.

3. Dodging Value-Talks

You can also tell that you're dealing with compromise when you notice the tendency to avoid discussions about ethics altogether. In high-pressure settings, people sometimes dodge "value talk" to avoid slowing down the process.

This can create a silent drift where decisions become more and more ethically ambiguous over time. When you notice that discussions are more focused on "getting it done" than on "doing it right," it's time to take a closer look.

Pressure has a way of creating a false sense of urgency that can overwhelm good judgment.

We often feel like there's simply no time for reflection or second-guessing. Every decision feels like it has to be made now. However, ethical shortcuts taken in haste can build up over time, eroding trust and integrity, both personally and within an organization.

Consider how small, seemingly harmless compromises add up. A team lead might cut corners to speed up a project once, then twice, and soon, it becomes the "standard approach." Or think about how an "everyone else is doing it" mentality can start to feel like a legitimate reason to follow suit.

It's easy to rationalize minor ethical lapses by pointing to the pace of the industry or the need to "keep up." But the more we give in to these justifications, the further we stray from our values.

In today's fast-paced markets, practices like arbitrage and differential pricing have become commonplace. On the surface, both strategies appear to serve reasonable business goals: arbitrage pricing corrects inefficiencies across markets, while differential pricing allows companies to maximize revenue by adjusting prices based on customer segments.

However, in our pursuit of profitability, we can easily let values slip, justifying excessive or exploitative practices with a simple "everyone else is doing it." This mentality, though widely accepted, often erodes the core values that businesses initially set out to uphold.

Arbitrage pricing, for instance, is traditionally seen as a mechanism for efficiency, where companies or individuals take advantage of price gaps across different markets. Yet, when taken to the extreme, it can be used to exploit less-informed buyers or create artificial scarcity, driving prices up without adding real value.

This excessive focus on profit over fairness undermines market integrity, shifting arbitrage from a beneficial strategy to a self-serving one. In a values-based framework, arbitrage should help balance markets and offer consumers fair prices, but when the "everyone else is doing it" mindset takes over, companies can find themselves justifying behavior that ultimately harms the marketplace and diminishes consumer trust.

Similarly, differential pricing is a widely accepted method where companies charge different prices based on factors like demand, location, or customer profile. While it can be an effective way to match consumer needs, it can also cross the line into discrimination or exclusion. For example, using algorithms to adjust prices dynamically may result in charging loyal or repeat customers higher prices purely because they are willing to pay.

The reasoning often boils down to "if it maximizes revenue, it's a fair game." Yet, this mindset overlooks the long-term impact on customer loyalty and brand reputation. Such businesses are gradually exposed to the risk of alienating their customers, as the value placed on customer relationships is replaced by an indiscriminate focus on the bottom line.

One final, often-overlooked sign that values may be slipping is when people avoid accountability. High-stakes environments can sometimes breed a "don't ask, don't tell" mentality.

If questions start to go unasked, if doubts are swept under the carpet, or if discussions start to avoid certain topics altogether, that's often a sign that something deeper is at play.

While this tendency is visible in high-stakes business environments, it is equally pervasive in our personal lives, shaping our habits, relationships, and even our self-perception. In day-to-day life, avoiding accountability can show up in subtle ways. For example, it could be blaming circumstances or others when things go wrong, hesitating to admit mistakes, or even turning a blind eye to actions that conflict with our values.

This avoidance often cultivates a "don't ask, don't tell" mentality, where we choose to ignore our own lapses or those of others to sidestep uncomfortable truths. These small acts of unaccountability accumulate, gradually shaping our character and affecting our relationships.

For example, in friendships, avoiding accountability can take the form of failing to address misunderstandings or hurt feelings. Instead of confronting issues openly, some may opt to gloss over tensions, hoping they'll resolve on their own.

This "don't ask, don't tell" approach may preserve harmony in the short term, but it often leads to resentment, eroded trust, and superficial connections.

When we avoid accountability in our relationships, we miss opportunities for

growth, honesty, and genuine connection, and
we ultimately compromise the depth and
authenticity of those bonds.

In our personal goals and self-discipline, the "don't ask, don't tell" mentality can show up as self-deception. For example, when we procrastinate on goals, neglect healthy habits, or fall short of our commitments, we might rationalize our actions with excuses. It becomes a pattern and can lead us to drift from the values we claim to hold dear, making it easier to settle for mediocrity rather than striving for integrity and self-improvement. Avoiding accountability here not only hinders personal growth but also sets a precedent for continued lapses in commitment as we become accustomed to letting ourselves off the hook.

Remember, integrity thrives in transparency. When discussions around accountability start to fade, it's a signal that values could be at risk.

Understanding the Cost of Compromised Values

The consequences of ethical compromise aren't always immediate, but they're inevitable. When values start to slip, so does trust. And trust, once lost, is difficult to regain. In fast-paced environments, a reputation for integrity can be one of the most valuable assets you hold. Teams, clients, and customers look to you and your organization for assurance that ethical standards will be upheld—even when it's not easy.

Imagine a healthcare provider that starts prioritizing profit over patient care due to financial pressures. Maybe they cut down on the time allotted for each patient, thinking it's a minor adjustment. But over time, patients feel rushed, care standards drop, and during all this, the trust erodes.

Suddenly, what started as a small compromise became a public relations crisis. This example isn't about judging anyone; it's about acknowledging the reality. Ethical decisions made under pressure can lead to a slippery slope. It is essential to recognize this before it spirals and there is not much you can do then to reverse the damage.

Ultimately, the bedrock of any lasting relationship is built on values—whether we're talking about relationships with clients, employees, or society at large.

Even though the cost of compromising values may not always be visible in the short run, it can leave lasting scars that impact not just individual careers but entire organizations.

Reflection as a Tool for Staying Grounded

So, it is only essential for you to understand how you can resist the pull toward compromise under pressure. Here's how. Start by making time for reflection, even in high-stakes situations. Just a few moments to pause, breathe, and ask yourself, "Is this aligned with my core values?" can make all the difference.

In practice, this can be as straightforward as taking five minutes at the start or end of each day to review decisions made and to reflect on how they sit with you. Reflection can feel illogical in fast-paced environments—like an added burden you can't afford. But these reflective moments are essential to maintain clarity. They help you reconnect with your core beliefs and give you a second chance to correct course when you might be drifting.

For example, let's say you're a manager who oversees a team under constant pressure to perform. By setting aside five minutes daily to reflect on your choices, you will be able to recognize patterns in your decision-making and adjust before slipping too far into reactive behavior.

Setting aside time for reflection does not mean slowing down the entire process; you only need to find that brief pause to check in with your values.

The Subtle Impact of Group Dynamics

The influence of group dynamics could have subtle impact and potentially sway value-driven decision-making in high-pressure environments. When everyone around you seems to be on board with a certain choice, even if it feels ethically ambiguous, it's natural to question your reservations.

Group pressure can create an unspoken expectation to conform, especially in close-knit, fast-paced teams that emphasize harmony and efficiency.

Think about a situation where a team is under intense pressure to deliver results quickly. If most members agree to bypass a standard procedure to save time, you might feel a subtle pull to go along with it, even if it doesn't sit right with you.

This doesn't mean the group is intentionally unethical. It just means the pressure has momentarily shifted their focus away from values and onto immediate solutions.

This is where it becomes essential to recognize the influence of groupthink. When groups face pressure, individual voices that would normally speak up tend to quiet down, and ethical concerns may be brushed aside for the sake of "keeping the peace."

If you feel uncomfortable with a group's direction, it's worth pausing to evaluate: are you sacrificing your values for the sake of unity? Are there ways to tactfully voice your concerns without disrupting the flow?

The Importance of Staying True to Your Own Ethical Compass

Navigating through ethical dilemmas often means drawing on an internal compass— more like a guardrail grounded in your core beliefs. It's not always easy to maintain, especially in settings where the collective drive for results can overshadow individual principles. Yet, holding steady to this compass can be a tremendous asset, not just for you but for everyone affected by your decisions.

So, what does it mean to stay true to your ethical compass under pressure?

First, it's about being honest with yourself regarding what feels right and wrong. If a situation feels off, it's worth paying attention to that gut instinct. Our intuition is often the first signal that values might be at risk, even if we don't yet have the words to explain why. Just a moment of quiet, honest reflection can often reveal the heart of an ethical issue.

Let's say you're working on a financial project where you're encouraged to take creative liberties with numbers to make the results appear more favorable. Your intuition may whisper that this is a line you shouldn't cross, even if others in your team insist it's "just the way things are done." Understand that the key here is to trust this inner guide, especially in high-stakes environments where the lines can get blurry.

Preserving Values in a Family Enterprise

I remember the story of a chief operating officer who protected the legacy values of her family's third-generation retail business by staying true to her own ethical compass.

The business was negotiating a partnership with a large conglomerate to expand its presence nationally. The deal looked incredible on paper, promising increased market share and a major boost in revenue.

However, during negotiations, the COO realized that the conglomerate planned to implement practices that conflicted with her family's core value of prioritizing local suppliers. The conglomerate wanted to centralize sourcing, which would have cut ties with the local producers who had been part of the business's ecosystem for decades.

Despite the constant pressure from other family members to close the deal, she stood her ground, explaining that the long-term success of the business was tied to the trust and loyalty of their local partners. Eventually, her persistence led to a restructured agreement that allowed the family business to retain control of its sourcing policies.

In a similar development, a chief executive officer in his family's agribusiness that has been built on transparency and ethical trade practices faced a defining moment. A large buyer offered a lucrative contract with a catch: they requested that the business inflate the reported quality of a product batch to secure export approvals.

While some family members saw this as a harmless adjustment, the CEO viewed it as a serious breach of trust. He convinced the family to reject the offer, arguing that their reputation for honesty was far more valuable than short-term gains. Though the decision resulted in an immediate financial hit, the business later attracted another major buyer who appreciated their transparency, securing a deal that exceeded the initial offer.

These stories hold very important lessons for professionals. Among other things, they show that standing firm, even when the numbers suggest otherwise, is sometimes necessary to protect values in business. Staying true to foundational principles can secure not just profits but trust and goodwill.

Furthermore, upholding values like honesty and transparency may come at a cost, but it also comes with a greater reward. It strengthens your reputation and attracts partners who align with your values.

The Power of Embracing Vulnerability

One of the most counterintuitive ways to navigate ethical dilemmas under pressure is to embrace vulnerability. High-pressure environments often promote a culture of toughness and control, leaving little room for moments of openness or doubt. But showing vulnerability—by admitting concerns or voicing uncertainty—can be a powerful way to align yourself with your values and create the opportunity for others to do the same.

Imagine a team meeting where the expectation is to agree on an immediate, perhaps ethically questionable solution. By courageously voicing your concerns, you create space for a more honest dialogue. Vulnerability here doesn't mean weakness; it means you're willing to stand for what feels right, even if it goes against the grain.

Sometimes, your openness can inspire others to voice their own hesitations, leading to a collective pause to reconsider.

This kind of vulnerability isn't easy, but it can be an incredibly effective way to prevent ethical missteps. When we allow ourselves to admit uncertainty, we invite others to explore alternatives and reevaluate hasty choices.

In doing so, vulnerability can actually strengthen the group's resolve to uphold shared values, even in fast-paced settings.

Decision-Making Frameworks for High-Stakes Ethical Choices

In moments of high-stakes decision-making, the pressure to act quickly can muddy our values and leave us grasping for the right course of action. That's where decision-making frameworks come in. These frameworks act as guiding lights, helping to simplify complex choices by anchoring them to ethical principles and a structured approach.

The goal isn't just to make a "good" decision; it's to make a decision you can stand by, one that aligns with your values and brings clarity to what might otherwise be a murky situation.

Building upon the principles that we established in the previous chapter, we'll explore some widely respected frameworks that prioritize ethical considerations. While these frameworks are often used in corporate or strategic settings, they're equally powerful when applied personally, especially in high-stakes scenarios. We'll discuss how they work and explore practical examples that show how you can apply them.

The Triple Bottom Line: Beyond Profit to People and Planet

In high-pressure environments, a structure's bottom line often becomes the primary focus. However, the Triple Bottom Line (TBL) framework urges decision-makers to look beyond profit alone.

Developed by John Elkington in the 1990s, TBL encourages leaders to assess the broader impact of their decisions by considering three elements: profit, people, and the planet. This approach widens the scope of traditional decision-making to include social and environmental effects, balancing financial outcomes with ethical responsibility.

Think about a scenario in the manufacturing sector where a team is deciding whether to cut costs by using cheaper materials that may harm the environment. Under TBL, the decision-making process doesn't end with profit margins.

The team must also evaluate how the change will affect the health of their employees and the surrounding community. Will the cheaper materials expose workers to hazardous conditions? Will the local environment suffer as a result? Taking these factors into account, the team has the chance to make a choice that considers financial success without compromising on ethical values.

Practical Application: Using TBL, you might evaluate a project's impact across these three dimensions with questions like:

- *Profit*: Is this financially sustainable in the long term, or is it a short-term gain that could damage future growth?

- *People*: Who will benefit from this choice, and who could be hurt by it? Does this decision respect stakeholders?

- *Planet*: What is the environmental cost, and can we mitigate any negative impact?

TBL systematically helps you see the broader implications of high-stakes decisions, offering a clearer path to balanced, ethically sound choices.

Stakeholder Analysis: Weighing Perspectives and Consequences

Stakeholder analysis is another powerful tool for ethical decision-making. At its core, this structure revolves around identifying all the parties affected by a decision and then evaluating the potential impact on each of them. Stakeholders can range from employees and clients to suppliers, local communities, and even future generations. It makes you consider the needs of each group and potential outcomes to make a more informed and ethically responsible decision.

Let's consider a common corporate dilemma: layoffs in the face of financial strain. A stakeholder analysis would lead you to look beyond the immediate impact on the bottom line. How will the layoffs affect employees and their families? What will be the community's response, especially if your company is a major local employer?

Examining the situation through the eyes of each stakeholder can help you gain more comprehensive insight into the impact of the decision. This allows you to weigh consequences more compassionately and responsibly.

Practical Application: To carry out a stakeholder analysis, start by mapping out all the groups affected by your decision. Then, ask questions such as:

• Who will benefit, and who may suffer as a result of this choice?

• What responsibilities do we have toward each group?

• How might this decision affect trust, loyalty, or long-term relationships with stakeholders?

When every stakeholder's perspective is considered, the decision may still be challenging, but you'll be able to approach it with greater clarity, ensuring you're not overlooking essential voices.

The Ethical Decision-Making Matrix: Balancing Choices with Values

The Ethical Decision-Making Matrix is a framework that helps clarify which values matter most in a given decision. The matrix is simple in structure: it's essentially a chart with possible options listed on one axis and core values on the other.

By systematically scoring or evaluating each option against your values, the matrix provides a structured approach to see which choice aligns most with your principles.

Imagine you're a leader in a technology firm, faced with the choice of developing software with limited privacy protections to meet a looming deadline. You could use an *Ethical Decision-Making Matrix* to rate each option against values like user privacy, transparency, product quality, and speed of delivery.

By scoring these options, you can quickly see which choice most closely aligns with your organizational and personal core values.

Practical Application: To use this matrix effectively:

1.   List the options available to you along one side.

2. On the adjacent side, identify core values relevant to the decision.

3. Evaluate each option based on how well it aligns with each value (e.g., on a scale of 1-5).

The table in the next page shows an example of what an ethical decision-making matrix might look like.

Decision Pillars	Stakeholder Impact	Alignment with Core Values (say Integrity)	Legal and Ethical Compliance	Short-Term Benefits	Long-Term Consequences	Ease of Implementation
Option A	High positive impact on employees, moderate on clients. **Score: 4**	Strong alignment with values. **Score: 5**	Fully compliant with legal/ethical standards. **Score: 5**	Moderate increase in revenue, high employee morale. **Score: 3**	High positive impact on reputation, low risk. **Score: 5**	Requires moderate effort achievable. **Score: 4**
Option B	Moderate positive impact on employees, high on clients. **Score: 3**	Partial alignment with values, high alignment with growth. **Score: 3**	Partially compliant, minor risk of ethical concerns. **Score: 3**	High revenue gain, moderate employee morale. **Score: 5**	Moderate risk to reputation, potential backlash. **Score: 3**	Low effort, easy implementation. **Score: 5**
Option C	Low positive impact on both employees and clients. **Score: 2**	Weak alignment, potential compromise on values. **Score: 2**	Fully compliant but raises ethical questions. **Score: 4**	Low revenue gain, potential decrease in employee morale. **Score: 2**	High risk to reputation, high potential for backlash. **Score: 1**	High effort, challenging implementation. **Score: 2**

Total Scores for Each Option:

- **Option A:** 26/30
- **Option B:** 22/30

- **Option C:** 13/30

Option A scores the highest overall, with strong alignment in key areas like stakeholder impact, core values, and long-term consequences. Its moderate effort in implementation is worth the balance it provides between ethical values and practical benefits.

Option B offers high short-term gains and is easy to implement but scores lower in ethical compliance and long-term impact, making it a more ethically ambiguous choice.

Option C has the lowest score, showing weak alignment with values and significant long-term risks. While it is legally compliant, its ethical compromises make it the least favorable choice.

Using this matrix, the scores provide a clearer, quantifiable view of how well each option aligns with both ethical principles and business objectives. This approach helps to make a decision based on a structured, value-centered analysis.

Integrating These Frameworks into High-Stakes Decisions

When you're under intense pressure, and the stakes are sky-high, incorporating these frameworks may feel like one more task in an already overwhelming situation. But the goal here isn't to add complexity. Instead, the goal here is to introduce structure, providing a compass that keeps you aligned with your values even when everything around you feels chaotic.

When facing a major decision, think of these frameworks as layers.

Start by considering the Triple Bottom Line, which gives you a high-level view of financial, social, and environmental impacts. Then, apply Stakeholder Analysis to zoom in on how each group is affected, providing a more nuanced understanding of the consequences. With these steps, you would gain a robust view of the ethical landscape, making it easier to find a path that aligns with both your immediate goals and your long-term principles.

Developing a Personal Framework for Ethical Decision-Making

While each framework provides guidance, there's immense value in crafting a personal approach that combines elements from each of them.

As time passes, you'll develop an intuitive judgment for which questions to ask, which priorities to weigh, and which values to protect. High-stakes environments can be unforgiving, so having a tailored approach to ethical decision-making is invaluable. It sets you apart in the business world.

Start by reflecting on which aspects of each framework resonate most with you. Are you drawn to the holistic perspective of the Triple Bottom Line? Or do you feel grounded by the individualized focus of stakeholder analysis?

Perhaps the clarity of a decision matrix appeals to you most. Blend these elements into a personal framework that feels natural. The goal is to develop a routine for ethical decision-making that remains steady, even under pressure.

As you refine your personal framework, remember that consistency matters.

The more often you apply your approach, the easier it will become to navigate through even the most challenging decisions with confidence. It will foster a sense of integrity that remains intact, regardless of the circumstances.

Please note that decision-making frameworks are not rigid rules; they're tools that help you stay rooted in your values, especially when the stakes are high.

While each approach has its strengths, it's the thoughtful combination of these tools that enables you to make decisions you can be proud of. By understanding the principles behind each framework and blending them into your decision-making process, you gain the flexibility to respond to complex ethical dilemmas with clarity and compassion.

Anyone can learn to make value-driven decisions.

Ethical dilemmas are complex, layered, and often wrapped in urgency that makes it difficult to pause and reflect. But as challenging as it is to plow through these situations, the rewards of staying aligned with your values are profound.

Value-driven decision-making is not just about avoiding mistakes; it's about building a reputation for integrity, gaining the trust of those around you, and creating a lasting impact.

By understanding the psychological and emotional impact of high-stakes situations, learning to spot common ethical conflicts, recognizing signs of compromise, and working with a proven framework, you can start to see these dilemmas with greater clarity.

Staying true to your own ethical compass, especially in the face of group dynamics and the pressures of urgency, will help you make choices that reflect not only what you want to achieve but also who you want to be.

In the end, value-driven decision-making is both a skill and a commitment.

It's the result of small, deliberate choices made consistently over time. As you regularly take a stand for your values, you will inspire others around you to do the same, especially those who look up to you as a leader.

You will come to realize that in high-stakes environments, true strength lies not in rushing to the finish line but in making decisions you can stand by long after the pressure fades.

5

POWER OF PERSONAL RESILIENCE AND INTEGRITY

What keeps us anchored to our values when the pressure builds? What keeps us grounded when the stakes are climbing and when the easiest choice would be to abandon our ethical principles?

In these moments, it is resilience that helps us to maintain our veracity and hold fast to our values. By strengthening our ability to stand firm and manage pressure, we build a foundation that does not shake or crumble under weight.

Integrity is the alignment of your actions with your values, even when no one is watching. It's the unwavering commitment to doing what's right, not because it's easy, but because it reflects the values you stand by.

Think of integrity as the adhesive that binds your beliefs to your behavior, creating consistency and trustworthiness. When you act with integrity, you're essentially saying, "This is who I am, and these are the principles I live by." Ensure that no matter what comes your way, you will not, under any circumstances, deviate from your principles.

Understand that it means you're not just reacting to external pressures or convenient outcomes but choosing actions rooted in a deeper sense of purpose and commitment to what is right. In moments of high stress or competing demands, integrity guides your choices, defining you as who you are and ensuring that they reflect your true values rather than the pressure of the moment.

In this chapter, we'll explore practices and perspectives that help build both resilience and integrity, giving you the tools to stay grounded when facing ethical challenges. We'll look at ways to strengthen personal ethics, manage stress, and draw inspiration from those who've upheld their values under extreme conditions.

A Practical Lesson on Aligning Actions with Personal Values

A frontline employee working in customer service for a multinational company, shared a defining moment in her career. She had been tasked with overseeing the internal queue system for processing customer requests, a role requiring both efficiency and discretion.

One day, a senior colleague approached her with a "special request." A high-ranking client wanted their request processed ahead of others waiting in line, and the senior colleague urged her to make it happen to maintain the relationship with this VIP. On the surface, it seemed like a harmless favor. And why wouldn't it when the company wouldn't lose money, and it might even strengthen ties with an important customer?

However, my friend realized the implications. Approving the request would compromise the fairness of the system, potentially undermining trust in the company's processes, especially among everyday customers who relied on them for transparency. Against mounting pressure from her colleague, she refused to prioritize the VIP request, explaining that fairness was a core value the company should uphold.

Her decision initially drew criticism, with some accusing her of being too rigid. But when news of her stance reached senior management, they commended her for standing by the company's principles. Her actions not only upheld fairness but also reinforced trust among customers, internal teams, and leadership alike.

What can we learn from this? Upholding fundamental values such as fairness, even in seemingly small decisions, builds trust and credibility within a system. We are more likely to make better decisions when we recognize the broader impact of our actions on organizational culture beyond short-term gains.

The Core of Resilience: Holding Firm to Your Principles

Resilience is more than just enduring hardships. It's about enduring without compromising what matters most. High-stakes situations often test this balance, making it tempting to bend or break personal principles to reach a quicker or easier outcome. But true resilience means holding steady to your values, especially when it's not convenient.

Think of a moment when you had to make a difficult choice when you could have chosen the easy way out. You may have felt isolated, uncertain, or even frustrated. Yet, by making the harder choice, you likely felt a sense of strength. That's resilience in action—a commitment to principles despite the discomfort or cost.

Building resilience starts with clarity.
Know your values.

If kindness, honesty, or responsibility matter to you, take time to understand what they look like in practice. In difficult moments, this clarity allows you to remember why you're holding firm. And in moments of temptation, it acts as a compass, reminding you that integrity isn't about what's easy; it's about what's lasting.

How to Develop Ethical Resilience

The process of developing resilience is like strength training; it's not a one-off event, and it doesn't happen overnight. It's a practice developed little by little through daily actions and small choices that align with your values.

Here are some disciplines to help you cultivate resilience in a sustainable, more practical way:

1. Self-Reflection: To stay true to your values, it is important to regularly reflect on them. Take time each day or week to consider your actions. Are they aligned with the values you hold dear? Reflection is like polishing a lens—it brings clarity and reminds you of what matters. Over time, this practice strengthens your resolve, giving you greater confidence to act with integrity even when under stress.

2. Setting Boundaries: Resilience is not about deliberately exposing yourself to high-pressure situations, thinking that you can withstand anything and everything. Rather, it's about recognizing limits and protecting them. Understand that challenging yourself to this extent can very easily backfire. Setting boundaries means you're creating space to prioritize what's important, whether it's time with family, focus on a project, or personal well-being.

When high-stakes situations arise, these boundaries become the guardrails that keep you safe. They help you to stand firm, even when things get tough.

Imagine you're managing a high-demand project with a tight deadline. It's tempting to work late nights or skip personal time to meet expectations. But by setting boundaries around your time, you ensure that you're at your best when it counts, which ultimately benefits both you and your work.

3. Practicing Self-Compassion: Building resilience requires self-compassion. There will be moments when you're tested, when things don't go as planned, or when you make a mistake. In these times, resilience means treating yourself with kindness. This is not self-indulgence. It's about acknowledging your humanity instead of playing the superhero. By doing this, you create a safe space to learn, recover, and recommit to your values.

These practices may seem simple, but they're incredibly powerful. Together, they create a resilient foundation that doesn't crack under pressure but grows stronger through every test.

Managing Stress and Finding Clarity

Stress is often the greatest threat to resilience. It clouds our thinking and makes it harder to stick to our values. Under stressful conditions, it's easy to make hasty decisions or to feel like you have no choice but to compromise. However, that isn't the case.

By learning to manage stress effectively,
you give yourself the space to think clearly and
act in alignment with your principles.

Consider a situation where you've been given a choice: approve a questionable expense or risk falling behind schedule. The stress of an impending deadline can make it tempting to bend the rules. But learning to manage stress allows you to pause, assess, and respond from a place of integrity.

Below are some helpful techniques for managing stress:

1. Mindful Breathing: Mindful breathing is a simple and immediate way to manage stress. When you feel pressure rising, pause and take a few deep breaths. Allow yourself five minutes to be away from the world. This short break gives you the chance to clear your mind, gain perspective, and reaffirm your commitment to your values.

2. Breaking Down Tasks: Some projects can feel overwhelming because of their sheer scope. Some of these projects may also be too lengthy to be coped with in the usual timeframe. Breaking down large tasks into manageable steps gives you control over the process, reduces anxiety, and helps you approach each part with focus and care. It's like building a puzzle one piece at a time; each small action moves you closer to a complete, value-aligned decision.

3. Physical Movement: Physical activity can release tension and provide mental clarity. A short walk, some light stretching, or even a quick moment to step away from your workspace can reset your stress levels and give you the focus needed to make clear, well-thought and, most importantly principled choices.

4. Sleep: Sleep is one of the most powerful techniques for managing stress and finding clarity. When you're well-rested, you're more resilient, focused, and better equipped to handle the pressures that can cloud your judgment. When you're under pressure, it's tempting to sacrifice sleep in favor of more work or preparation, but this often backfires.

Without sufficient rest, stress can feel amplified, and it's harder to think clearly, stay calm, or make decisions aligned with your values.

Quality sleep helps your body system to regulate emotions, replenish mental energy, and reinforce your ability to stand by your ethical commitments.

Prioritizing rest protects your health and keeps you sharp, so you can make thoughtful, values-driven decisions even under pressure.

Integrating these practices into your life and work will help to reduce stress while also increasing your capacity for clear, value-driven decisions. When you're able to stay calm and focused, your resilience grows, allowing you to handle even the most challenging moments with integrity.

Drawing Inspiration from Leaders Who Upheld Their Values

Let history teach you a lesson. Throughout history, we've seen individuals who maintained their values under extraordinary pressure. These examples can serve as inspiration, reminding us that resilience and integrity are achievable, even in the most difficult situations. Let's consider three examples.

1. Rosa Parks and the Courage to Stand Firm

Rosa Parks' refusal to give up her bus seat is often celebrated as a pivotal moment in civil rights history. But it's easy to forget the pressure she faced at that moment. She risked personal safety, public criticism, and legal consequences.

Yet, in the face of these risks, she held firm to her beliefs, becoming a symbol of strength and courage. Her story shows that resilience is about having the courage to choose what's right over what's easy, even when the stakes are painfully high.

2. Nelson Mandela and the Power of Perseverance

Mandela's 27 years in prison tested his resilience and commitment to equality. He endured hardships, isolation, and intense pressure to abandon his ideals. Yet, through this, Mandela remained committed to his values, demonstrating that true resilience isn't just about surviving challenges. He showed us that it's about remaining true to your beliefs, no matter how difficult the journey. His story reminds us that personal integrity is a source of strength that can outlast even the most oppressive circumstances.

3. HR Officer's Commitment to Diversity, Equity, and Inclusion

An HR officer in a mid-sized tech company faced a challenging situation when recruiting for a senior developer position. After weeks of interviews, the team shortlisted two candidates: a highly qualified female developer and a male candidate with slightly less experience but a referral from an influential company board member.

In a meeting to finalize the hire, the board member strongly advocated for his candidate, emphasizing the importance of "maintaining harmony" in a male-dominated team. The numbers were compelling, as the male candidate's connections and network could bring in new business opportunities.

However, the HR officer believed in the company's commitment to diversity and equal opportunity. She presented objective data supporting the female candidate who was equally qualified with relatively equal network capacity. The officer argued that hiring her would not only promote inclusivity but also enhance the team's technical expertise.

Despite facing considerable resistance, her insistence on fairness won out. The female candidate was hired and went on to exceed performance expectations, ultimately becoming a team leader who drove innovation and mentorship for younger employees.

Becoming a Value-Driven Leader Under Pressure

The stories of Rosa Parks, Nelson Mandela, and the HR officer remind us that resilience is possible, even when it seems impossible. By staying connected to our values, we can handle even the most challenging situations with purpose and strength.

As you strengthen your resilience, remember that the goal is not perfection—it's progress. Becoming a value-driven leader under pressure is not about getting it right every time; it's about learning, adapting, and recommitting to your values with each new challenge.

When you are confronted with situations that test your integrity, reflect on what you've learned and ask yourself how you can use those lessons to become stronger. Turn the pressure into an opportunity to grow, learn, and become a better leader.

Resilience as the Foundation of Integrity

Building resilience is like fortifying the foundation of a house, for it holds up everything in one place. When you take time to nurture this quality, you create a personal structure that can weather any storm. High-stakes situations will come, but with resilience, you're prepared to face them with integrity and strength.

Remember that resilience is not about being perfect; it's about being present, staying committed, and continually growing. With self-reflection, setting boundaries, managing stress, getting sufficient sleep, and drawing inspiration from exemplary figures, you strengthen your ability to lead with integrity, no matter the pressures you face. This way, you ensure that you face any challenge comes your way without deviating from the principles you abide by.

6

WHAT SHAPES OUR VALUES?

Values are deeply rooted in who we are and how we perceive the world. They aren't just surface-level beliefs we pick up in passing—they're woven into our identities, our choices, and, ultimately, our work. Understanding where values come from can reveal why they resonate so strongly with us and why they hold such significance in the decisions we make.

This chapter explores how personal experiences, family influences, and cultural backgrounds shape our values, making them a powerful, though often hidden, force in decision-making.

The Foundation of Personal Values

Think of a time when you were a kid. Were there lessons that you learned as you grew up? Of course, there were early lessons you absorbed in childhood. Did you ever take a moment out of your day and reflect on what those lessons could be and how they shape you today? Maybe one of the lessons was the importance of honesty, the rewards of hard work, or the need for compassion. These early impressions are often instilled by family, mentors, or close community members, forming the building blocks of our personal value system. While they might not be obvious in every decision we make, these values form an invisible framework that guides us, especially when we face ethical or complex decisions.

Picture an entrepreneur who grew up in a family where hard work was everything. That belief in diligence will likely impact their approach to business, driving them to prioritize work ethic and resilience in their own company culture. It might mean they view every setback as temporary, just another challenge to work through.

Or think about someone who grew up valuing community. This person is likely to make business decisions that take a broader, more inclusive view, considering the ripple effects of their actions on employees, customers, and the local community.

These foundational values don't just affect our actions; they influence how we interpret success and values.

The standards you grew up with may even subconsciously define what "winning" means to you. For some, winning may mean financial achievement; for others, it's about the positive impact they make. While these values tend to take the front seat in our lives without us even realizing it, understanding them to their basic core can help us use them mindfully to our own advantage. And as we'll see, understanding where our values come from is the first step in wielding them intentionally in our professional lives.

How Culture Shapes Our Beliefs and Judgments

Culture has a broader scope than you might perceive it to have. It plays a pivotal role in shaping values on a much larger scale. The cultural environment we grow up in, the norms of it that we are introduced to and continue to mingle with for years— its heroes, its shared history, are the factors that tell us what's celebrated and what's discouraged.

In many Western cultures, for example, values like individualism, ambition, and innovation are often highlighted, whereas in some Eastern cultures, values like community, harmony, and tradition are more prominent. This shows that values have the potential to vary depending on the surroundings in which they are rooted.

These cultural influences may not define us completely, but they give us a framework, a societal "language" of values that becomes part of our worldview.

Imagine a leader from a collectivist culture. Perhaps they're from a place where the good of the group takes precedence over individual desires. In the workplace, they might instinctively make decisions that prioritize team cohesion, often going to great lengths to ensure everyone feels included and respected.

On the other hand, a leader from a culture that celebrates individual achievement might emphasize personal accountability and innovation, valuing unique contributions that set the organization apart.

In a globalized world, these cultural distinctions create both challenges and opportunities. Business leaders today frequently work across cultural boundaries, making it crucial to understand not only their own values but also those of others.

Awareness of these differences can prevent misunderstandings, encouraging collaboration built on mutual respect. As companies become increasingly multicultural, this cultural understanding becomes a vital asset in creating an inclusive and effective work environment.

Family Influence: The First Source of Our Values

Family, often our first community, provides some of the strongest value-based lessons we have ever received. Early family experiences are where most of us learn about loyalty, respect, empathy, and, perhaps most importantly, accountability. These values might be instilled through direct lessons—like a parent teaching us to respect others—or indirectly through examples, like witnessing a family member's dedication to their work.

Consider someone raised in a family of entrepreneurs who placed high value on perseverance and adaptability. This person may carry forward a strong belief in these qualities, viewing flexibility and resilience as essential in any business venture.

Or think of someone who grew up in a household where service to others was prioritized. That upbringing might lead them to establish a business model that incorporates a social mission, ensuring that their work benefits more than just the bottom line.

Family influences are powerful because they shape us when we're most impressionable.

They form an internal compass that often continues to guide us, consciously or not, throughout our careers. This compass doesn't dictate every decision that we make, but it does serve as a source of guidance when we find ourselves at a crossroads of moral dilemmas. When we are faced with ethical questions or complex choices, these values provide us with a direction, ensuring that we make the right choice.

Even when we don't actively consider these family-rooted values, they're often there in the background, influencing our judgment and shaping our approach to both personal and professional challenges.

Personal Experiences: The Unique Influence of Our Journeys

While family and culture set the stage, our personal experiences add a unique, individual layer to our values. Significant events—successes, failures, relationships, and crises—all contribute to how we perceive the world and the values we hold dear.

An entrepreneur who's faced financial hardship may value security and stability, making conventional financial decisions in their business. Meanwhile, someone who has benefited from mentorship early in their career may prioritize education and growth, often going out of their way to invest in their employees' development.

These individual experiences allow values to evolve. They might reinforce the values we grew up with or introduce new ones.

For instance, an executive who has witnessed corporate misconduct may become a staunch advocate for transparency and ethics. This doesn't mean they weren't ethical before; rather, their experience strengthened and clarified a commitment to integrity that they carry into every decision.

Personal experiences add a sense of urgency and authenticity to our values. When you've lived through a hardship or a success, your values don't just become something you believe in; they become a core part of your identity. They drive you to act with purpose, knowing that your decisions align with who you truly are. And when leaders bring this authenticity into their work, they inspire the same sense of purpose in those around them.

Personal vs. Organizational Values: Define If You Fit In

A close friend of mine once shared a defining experience that deeply shaped his understanding of values in professional settings.

Sometime in the early days of his career, he accompanied a managing partner to negotiate a financial advisory engagement at a client's office. Everything was going smoothly, and they were on the verge of closing the deal when the client made an unexpected request.

The client wanted them to inflate their professional fees by about 5%, essentially as a bribe. Without hesitation, the managing partner declined, stating that their firm did not operate that way.

The client, obviously displeased, threatened to withhold the contract, implying that they weren't willing to "play the game." In response, the managing partner simply closed his laptop, turned to my friend, and calmly said, "Let's go."

Years later, my friend found himself in a leadership role as the finance lead in another organization, where he was responsible for evaluating business transactions. While reviewing proposals from the marketing and sales teams, he noticed something troubling.

Almost all the proposals included "facilitation fees"—essentially inflated costs intended to meet financial requests from clients. In most cases, these costs are added back to the project cost and borne by the client. It seemed to be an unspoken norm in that environment, an expected part of doing business.

My friend resisted, advocating for an approach that aligned with ethical business practices. However, his stance put him at odds with team leads who had grown accustomed to seeing such fees as standard procedure virtually for all their transactions.

Reflecting on these experiences, he shared a profound observation about the erosion of professional values. When questionable practices like facilitation fees become normalized, particularly for young professionals who are introduced to them as routine, the lines of ethical behavior become dangerously blurred. It left him pondering a critical question: Who sets the boundaries of values in such environments?

My friend's experience illustrates that each organization has its own distinctive set of values. As a professional, it is important to always reflect on how your experiences have shaped your values. Then, take a step further to assess if there is an alignment between your personal values and the values prioritized in your workplace.

In environments where ethics are compromised, standing firm in your values is essential, but if there is no support system in terms of leadership and policy enforcement, it can be difficult to thrive. Always think about the downstream impact of any values-based decision. Be wise about how you choose your values to come into play.

The Intersection of Personal and Cultural Values in Decision-Making

In the world of business, decisions are rarely simple. They involve layers of considerations, and our personal and cultural values add complexity to that decision-making process. In many ways, values serve as the foundation of our intuition. The "gut feelings" we get in situations that put our values to the test originate from the values that we have built over time. Remember that these gut feelings guide us when the data is unclear or when the stakes are high.

When leaders understand the origins of their values, they can better appreciate how those values affect their decisions.

For example, if a leader values independence due to their cultural background, they may instinctively favor decentralized decision-making, empowering employees to take initiative. Meanwhile, a leader who values community may emphasize collaboration and team cohesion, ensuring that decisions reflect group consensus.

Balancing personal values with cultural expectations isn't always easy, especially in diverse teams.

Leaders who are conscious of these intersections—who recognize their own values and those of others—are often better equipped to create inclusive, respectful environments where varied perspectives can thrive. This awareness allows for richer decision-making, grounded in a blend of insights that respect both individual and collective values.

The Power of Self-Awareness in Leading with Values

Ultimately, recognizing the roots of our values equips us with self-awareness, an invaluable tool in leadership. When you are self-aware, you understand that your values shape not just your decisions but also how others perceive you. You know that when you act in alignment with your core beliefs, you project authenticity and inspire trust. Conversely, when you compromise these values, you risk creating a disconnect and uncertainty within your team. Understand that there well may be short-term results, successes even. However, in the longer run, you are bound to face difficulties for not abiding by core values that keep you from crossing a line and doing something that goes against ethical practices.

Self-awareness also enables you to embrace
value-driven decision-making confidently,
even when it challenges conventional norms.

When you are clear on the origins of your values, you become more resilient in the face of external pressures to compromise. You can stand firm in your beliefs, knowing that your decisions are grounded in something deeper than mere profitability or compliance.

In this way, values become a source of strength, guiding you to make choices that reflect not only what is practical but also what is right. And as we'll continue to discover, this commitment to values isn't just good for personal integrity; it's good for business, too.

Embracing the Diversity of Values

In today's global business landscape, embracing the diversity of values is not just beneficial—it's essential. As teams and markets become more diverse, successful leaders recognize that no single value set can address every challenge. Instead, they cultivate an environment where different values can coexist, complementing each other and enriching the organization's collective wisdom.

When leaders approach value-driven decisions with openness, they allow for a range of perspectives that can inspire innovation, inclusivity, and resilience. This approach doesn't dilute their own values; it strengthens them, creating a shared purpose that is inclusive, adaptive, and responsive to the needs of a globalized world.

In the end, understanding the origins of our values—personal, cultural, and experiential—empowers us to lead with empathy, integrity, and confidence. It reminds us that values are more than ideals; they're the legacy we leave in the lives we impact and the work we create.

7

CAN VALUES BE RIGHT OR WRONG?

Values guide us through our choices in business and in life, but who decides which values are "right" and which are "wrong?"

There is no universal answer here. In fact, this is far more complex, layered, and often subjective, especially in the increasingly globalized and interconnected world that we live in today.

While some values—like honesty and integrity—are universally respected, others are shaped by personal beliefs, experiences, cultural nuances, and societal expectations that can vary significantly from one person or place to the next. So, who sets these boundaries, and on what grounds?

In this chapter, we'll explore the origins and conflicts around defining "right" and "wrong" values in the professional sphere and how understanding these nuances can empower us to make more intentional, informed decisions.

As we dig into this, keep in mind that values aren't always clear-cut. Sometimes, they're as much about context as they are about ethics, and the boundary between "right" and "wrong" can be a moving target.

Universal vs. Relative Values: A Complex Balance

Some values have universal appeal. They're principles we'd likely all agree on as essential. Integrity, honesty, and respect. These principles serve as the cornerstones of trust, and without trust, business crumbles.

Most of us would agree that a company that treats its employees with respect and ensures to provide a better working environment tends to thrive more as compared to organizations that are driven by profit and profit alone. Employees, when they feel valued, they tend to do work with more dedication than in an environment where their needs take a backseat. More so, such companies prove to value not just their employees but also their customers. Hence, the customers feel safe and respected, reinforcing loyalty and trust.

These universal values create a baseline, a sort of unspoken agreement that binds us all together, regardless of culture, background, or industry.

However, when we dig deeper, the waters get murkier. Outside of these universal ideals, we encounter values that can differ sharply depending on cultural or regional norms. Consider the value of individualism versus collectivism.

In many Western cultures, individualism—the idea that personal achievement and self-expression should be prioritized—is often celebrated and even expected. Yet, in other parts of the world, collectivism takes precedence, with greater emphasis on group harmony and community over individual gain.

This doesn't mean one is inherently right and the other wrong; it's a matter of perspective.

In a collective culture, a business leader might prioritize team decisions and consensus over rapid innovation driven by individual achievement.

On the other hand, in a more individualistic environment, innovation and autonomy may take precedence, with success defined by personal accomplishment and pioneering ideas.

Both approaches can lead to success, yet they embody contrasting values—each meaningful in its own context.

Let's consider two successful business leaders who embody different values and approaches to success. The example focuses on Warren Buffett and Elon Musk. Warren Buffett is known for his emphasis on long-term value and prudent financial management. He focuses on stability, patience, and investment in businesses with strong fundamentals.

His value system prioritizes ethical stewardship, risk aversion, and sustainable growth, often describing his investments as "forever" holdings. Buffett's approach reflects values of stability, tradition, and long-term security.

In contrast, Elon Musk exemplifies the values of innovation and aggressive risk-taking. His focus is on disrupting industries—from electric vehicles to space exploration—often with audacious timelines and bold promises.

Musk values speed, radical thinking, and pushing boundaries, even if that sometimes means taking on significant risks and encountering public criticism. His approach speaks of the values of exploration, disruption, and rapid, transformative change.

Buffett's approach values conservatism and steady growth, while Musk thrives on rapid innovation and high-stakes risks. Both have achieved remarkable success but operate from fundamentally different values.

This shows how diverse values can shape different paths to accomplishment, with each approach being right in its own context.

The Influence of Industry Standards and Corporate Culture

Values don't just arise from personal or cultural beliefs—they're also heavily influenced by industry standards and the culture within organizations themselves.

In finance, transparency and accountability might be the gold standard, while in tech, innovation and disruption are often the key values shaping daily decisions. What's right in one industry might be wrong, or at least questionable, in another. This also applies to companies within the same industry.

Let's take an example of two tech companies. One places high value on speed and disruption; it encourages a culture where "failing fast" is part of the innovation process. Here, a project that doesn't pan out isn't necessarily a failure—it's part of the learning curve.

Another company that values stability and long-term thinking may find this "fail-fast" culture reckless, preferring to invest in projects that are carefully tested and less risky. Both companies could be successful yet operate under very different value systems.

These contrasting value orientations aren't random; they're driven by the unique demands and expectations within each industry.

This interplay between values and industry norms raises questions about how flexible values should be and to what extent they should adapt—

or hold firm—under the influence of professional standards.

The Role of Leadership in Shaping Values

Leadership plays a crucial role in setting and reinforcing values within an organization. Leaders not only communicate expected behaviors but also embody the values they wish to see in others. A company's leadership establishes boundaries on what's "acceptable" or "right" within its own walls, effectively setting the tone for the entire culture.

A leader who advocates for sustainability demonstrates a strong commitment to environmental responsibility, indicating that sustainable practices are a fundamental, non-negotiable value. On the other hand, a leader focused primarily on maximizing profits may create a culture where results are prioritized over environmental or ethical considerations.

Each decision reflects a value judgment, subtly or explicitly setting boundaries on what is considered right or wrong in the organization.

However, leaders don't operate in a vacuum. They're influenced by the stakeholders around them, from shareholders to employees and even customers. Each group brings its own set of expectations and values, and leaders must relate to them appropriately to foster a coherent culture.

Nevertheless, the best leaders don't simply adopt values based on pressure or trends. They clarify their own values and model them consistently, building a framework that aligns with the company's mission and vision while also meeting the needs and expectations of their stakeholders.

The Ethical Dilemma: Can Values Be Wrong?

Let's address an uncomfortable question: can a value be "wrong"? Some would argue that as long as a value aligns with the goals of the organization and doesn't cause harm, it's valid. However, the issue becomes more complex when certain values lead to ethically questionable actions, especially when profit is involved.

Consider the case of a company that prioritizes profit maximization above all else. While profitability is a necessary and often laudable goal, making it the sole driving value can lead to questionable practices, such as cost-cutting that sacrifices employee well-being or prioritizing short-term gains over long-term impact.

Here, the pursuit of profit as an isolated value becomes problematic, potentially leading to actions that, while not illegal, may be considered unethical or "wrong" in a broader societal context.

The challenge is that business doesn't exist in a vacuum. The impact of decisions often extends beyond the company itself, affecting employees, communities, and sometimes even global ecosystems. A value that seems right within an organization might appear wrong when viewed through a larger lens.

This brings us back to the need for balance and the realization that while not all values are universally "wrong," some may require reassessment when they conflict with ethical considerations or societal norms.

Balancing Customer Satisfaction and Employee Safety

A close friend who worked as an operations manager at a logistics company shared a time when she had to make a tough call regarding customer demands. A major client required an urgent delivery during severe weather conditions.

Meeting the deadline would maintain the company's high customer satisfaction ratings and prevent financial penalties. However, fulfilling the request would require dispatching drivers on potentially hazardous routes.

When she consulted her team, many were reluctant but felt pressured to proceed, knowing the company valued its client relationships highly. My friend decided to prioritize her drivers' safety over the client's demands.

She informed the client that the delivery would be delayed due to safety concerns and offered alternative solutions, such as partial shipments or digital access to critical documents.

Though the client expressed frustration initially, they later appreciated the company's transparency and employee-first approach. The operation manager's decision also strengthened trust within her team, as the drivers felt valued and protected. This experience became a defining moment in the company's culture, emphasizing the importance of employee well-being alongside customer satisfaction.

While customer obsession is commendable, it is equally important to maintain a balance by prioritizing employee safety. You can build a motivated workforce when employees feel cared for.

Addressing the Gray Areas

If values were black and white, decisions would be easy. But as we know, they rarely are. Value-based decisions often land in gray areas, where boundaries blur, and there's no clear "right" answer.

In these situations, understanding the context becomes essential. Sometimes, it's less about determining a right or wrong value and more about recognizing which values should take precedence in a specific situation.

Consider a scenario where a company must decide whether to prioritize speed to market or product safety. In a competitive landscape, speed is critical if a company must stay ahead, but safety is equally important.

Here, the values of innovation and responsibility come into direct conflict. A "right" answer might not be immediately clear, and the decision requires weighing the potential consequences of each path.

This is where value-driven leaders truly shine. They don't rely on absolutes; instead, they draw on their own values and the values of their team to steer through complex situations.

They ask questions, seek diverse perspectives, and remain open to challenging their own assumptions. By doing so, they find a path forward that aligns not only with business goals but also with the ethical standards that guide their actions.

The Role of Internal and External Accountability

In today's world, organizations are accountable not only to themselves and their shareholders but also to the wider public. Social media, transparency regulations, and consumer expectations place businesses under constant scrutiny, amplifying the importance of aligning with broadly accepted values.

For example, a company's commitment to social responsibility can be a powerful asset—or a significant risk—depending on how consistent and authentic that commitment is perceived to be.

External pressures remind companies that beyond serving as internal guides, values also have a public impact.

Missteps or misalignments with publicly accepted values can lead to backlash, whether through consumer boycotts, regulatory penalties, or reputational harm. While this may seem limiting, it also presents an opportunity. Accountability nurtures integrity, prompting businesses to commit more deeply to values that benefit both their interests and the wider community.

Embracing the Complexity of Values in Business

In the end, setting boundaries around "right" and "wrong" values in business is not about following a strict rulebook. It's about understanding the complex layers of personal beliefs, cultural norms, industry expectations, and ethical standards. It's about recognizing contradictions and making informed, intentional choices that reflect not only what's practical but also what aligns with a broader sense of purpose.

Values don't have to be perfect or universally agreed upon. They need to be genuine, thoughtful, and aligned with the impact you want to create.

The goal is not to avoid challenging values but to approach them with clarity and confidence, knowing that each decision is an opportunity to reinforce the legacy you want to build.

As we move forward, let's keep questioning, learning, and growing in our understanding of values. And let's remember that while values may not always be easy to define or uphold, they're the compass that guides us through every decision, shaping our work, our impact, and ultimately, our world.

8

HOW EXPERIENCE AFFECTS VALUE JUDGMENTS

How often do we stop to consider the role our personal experiences play in shaping our values? As we encounter various situations and challenges, the perspectives we gain become the lens through which we evaluate what's important and, ultimately, the decisions we make.

In a business setting, where values can influence everything from workplace culture to financial strategy, the impact of personal perspective is profound—and often underestimated. Recognizing this connection between experience and values is essential for leaders who want to foster better understanding, empathy, and sound decision-making in our continuously evolving, complex world.

This chapter discusses in detail how experiences shape our values and how, in turn, these values shape our actions. You'll also discover the unique factors that mold each of us and how acknowledging these influences can create more thoughtful and impactful choices.

Experience as the Foundation of Personal Values

From a young age, our experiences start to carve out the values that will guide us throughout life. Imagine two individuals: one grows up in a competitive environment, learning that success requires fierce ambition and resilience. On the other hand, the other is raised in a community where cooperation and shared effort are prized.

Both sets of experiences will shape different core values—perhaps one will prioritize personal achievement, while the other might prioritize teamwork and shared success.

In the business world, these foundational experiences affect how we interpret and apply values in our professional lives. A leader who values ambition might encourage their team to push boundaries and embrace risk.

On the other hand, a leader who values collaboration may focus on developing a supportive environment that emphasizes group success over individual rewards and praises. Both approaches have their strengths, yet they emerge from very different experiences and perspectives.

It's not that one approach is right or wrong. Rather, it's about understanding where these values come from and how they influence our actions.

The Subjectivity of Value Judgments

Values are personal beliefs that everyone holds, which means they can vary greatly from person to person. What one person values may be completely different from what someone else values, making values subjective. What is really important to one person might not mean much to someone else. This difference usually reflects the unique experiences that have influenced how each person sees the world.

For example, someone who has worked in an environment marked by constant change might highly value adaptability and flexibility, seeing them as essential for success. Whereas someone with a background in a highly regulated industry might value stability and consistency, viewing them as non-negotiable for achieving long-term goals.

This subjectivity doesn't make one perspective more valuable than another. Instead, it highlights the diversity of viewpoints that individuals bring to the table. And while this diversity can sometimes lead to tension, it can also drive innovation and resilience when people come together with open minds and mutual respect.

Consider a situation where two department heads disagree on how to allocate resources: one advocates for aggressive investment in new technologies. At the same time, the other pushes for a cautious approach that favors the maintenance of current operations.

Their difference in perspective likely stems from past experiences—one may have witnessed rapid success through innovation, while the other has seen the risks of overextension. By acknowledging the unique perspectives each person brings, they can arrive at a balanced decision that leverages both values.

How Perspective Shapes Leadership Style

As leaders, our perspectives heavily influence the decisions we make and how we interact with our teams. Experience teaches us, subtly or overtly, what works and what doesn't, shaping our personal philosophy and guiding our leadership style.

A leader who has risen through the ranks by taking calculated risks may encourage a culture of experimentation, valuing innovation and flexibility. On the other hand, a leader who understands the risks of too much ambition might focus more on stability. They could prefer being careful and making detailed plans instead of taking big, risky actions.

The different styles of leadership come from the unique experiences each leader has had in their life. However, the best leaders understand that their point of view is just one of many. They are open to seeing things from different perspectives. They know that to make well-rounded decisions, they must tap into the diverse perspectives within their teams.

This openness to different viewpoints fosters a richer, more inclusive environment where ideas can flourish and value judgments are shaped collaboratively rather than imposed.

When leaders embrace a variety of perspectives, they also set an example for their teams. They show that values aren't rigid or prescriptive; rather, they are adaptable and open to growth. This willingness to integrate different experiences and viewpoints encourages team members to bring their authentic selves to work, knowing that their unique perspectives are valued and respected.

The Influence of Cultural Backgrounds

In Chapter 6, we discussed in detail how culture shapes our beliefs and judgment. This is profound in influencing how we view the world and our interaction with it. Just as personal experiences shape individual values, cultural backgrounds influence the collective values within an organization. Cultural norms and societal expectations impact how individuals perceive and prioritize values, often creating shared perspectives that can either align or clash with other groups.

In many cultures, showing respect for authority and following a chain of command are important values. In these cultures, people often prioritize being loyal and showing respect to their elders or those in higher positions at work. In contrast, cultures that value egalitarianism might prioritize open dialogue and equality, encouraging team members to challenge ideas regardless of the speaker's position.

These cultural influences shape how people approach their work, interact with colleagues, and define success.

Managing cultural differences calls for awareness and sensitivity. Leaders who understand the role of cultural background in value formation can create an environment where diverse perspectives are celebrated rather than stifled.

They recognize that while values may vary, each perspective adds value to the collective mission. By encouraging cultural awareness, leaders build bridges between individuals and groups, creating a more cohesive and adaptable organization.

Challenging Our Own Biases

The most challenging part of value-based decision-making is recognizing that our own perspectives are not absolute. Often, our experiences create biases that color our judgment, leading us to favor certain values over others without fully considering alternative viewpoints.

Recognizing this bias is a powerful step toward becoming more balanced and adaptable.

Daniel, managed a consulting team where precision was his core value, and every client report had to be meticulously fact-checked, formatted, and error-free. He believed credibility came from perfection.

One of his top analysts, Tunde, valued flexibility. He believed that speed and adaptability mattered more than perfect details, especially in fast-moving client engagements. If a client needed quick insights, he prioritized delivering a strong draft over refining every minor detail.

Tension arose when a major client requested a presentation within 24 hours. Daniel insisted that every data point be re-verified before submission. Tunde, however, believed a solid first draft was better than a delayed perfect version. Despite their differing values, the presentation was delivered. Tunde got it out on time, and Daniel reviewed key details at the last minute. The client was satisfied, but their debate continued.

In the end, they never fully agreed, but they learned to balance each other—Daniel ensuring quality, and Tunde keeping the team agile. Their values clashed, yet the work got done.

This isn't to say we should abandon our values. In fact, let's hold onto our values firmly while embracing a constructive and adaptive approach that encourages us to learn from others. By staying open to different perspectives, we can grow and improve together. By challenging our biases, we gain a fuller picture of the values at play and become more effective in making inclusive, well-rounded decisions.

Perspective and Empathy in Decision-Making

When we recognize that values stem from experience, we also become more empathetic in our decision-making. Empathy allows us to understand where others are coming from, even when their values differ from our own. It helps us move beyond judgment and embrace the richness of diverse perspectives.

Daniel and Tunde are classic examples of how empathy allows each member to appreciate the reasoning behind the other's stance rather than seeing it as an obstacle.

By understanding the motivations that shape each person's perspective, the team can find a solution that respects both efficiency and quality, creating a balanced approach that honors everyone's values.

Empathy does not imply compromising our values; rather, it entails understanding them in relation to those of others.

It's about seeking to understand before seeking to be understood. This creates a foundation of mutual respect, ultimately leading to stronger outcomes that are more aligned with our values.

Embracing Growth and Evolving Values

One of the most profound aspects of perspective is that it evolves. As we gather new experiences, our values can shift, sometimes dramatically. What we once held as essential may become less so, replaced by values that better reflect our current stage in life or career.

This evolution is natural and healthy, yet it can be unsettling. Embracing growth in our values requires humility and openness. It requires the willingness to acknowledge that we don't have all the answers and that learning is a lifelong journey. It means realizing that change is not a betrayal of our previous convictions but a sign of advancement and a reflection of the adaptability that characterizes strong leaders and resilient organizations.

Consider a professional who once valued financial success above all else but, through life's challenges, comes to value work-life balance and meaningful impact more. This shift doesn't invalidate their previous values. Understand that it simply reflects a new perspective shaped by lived experience. Recognizing and embracing these changes allows individuals to stay true to themselves while evolving with the demands and realities of their personal and professional lives.

Prioritizing Competing Commitments

A sales manager in a hospitality business recounted her approach to balancing family commitments with demanding work schedules. The business had introduced an overtime allowance to keep up with peak season demand. While most employees, including her, were tempted to maximize their income, she began to notice how her long hours were affecting her relationship with her children.

Realizing that her constant absence was creating distance in her family, she made a deliberate choice to set boundaries. She restructured her work schedule, delegating tasks to team members and prioritizing weekends for family time. Though she missed out on significant financial incentives, she later shared how her strengthened family bonds became the real reward.

A director in a manufacturing firm faced a similar challenge. His company had landed a big project with short deadlines, promising workers, including him, a substantial bonus for putting in extra hours. For months, he worked late nights, skipping family dinners and missing his daughter's school events.

One evening, his daughter asked why he was never home, saying she missed spending time with him. Her words hit him hard, and he decided to make a change. He spoke with his team, delegated tasks, and committed to leaving work on time at least three days a week. While he earned a smaller bonus, he found greater fulfillment in being present for his family.

As much as we desire to maximize our earnings, it is important to recognize that money can be replaced, but moments with loved ones cannot. Setting boundaries not only enriches personal relationships but also improves mental well-being and long-term productivity.

No financial incentive can replace the value of being there for your loved ones. Delegation and time management are powerful strategies to maintain both professional and personal commitments.

Building a Culture that Celebrates Diverse Experiences

Ultimately, understanding the influence of perspective on value judgments in a business setting is about creating a culture where diverse experiences are not only acknowledged but also celebrated. It's about encouraging individuals to bring their full selves to work, knowing that their exceptional perspective is valued and that they contribute meaningfully to the collective mission.

Organizations that prioritize this inclusive approach find themselves better prepared to manage complexity and change.

They benefit from a workforce that's not only skilled but also deeply committed to shared goals because each individual's values have a place within the larger framework. By creating a culture where diverse perspectives inform values, leaders can build a resilient, adaptable organization that's well-equipped to face both current and future challenges.

9

VALUES IN TECHNOLOGY AND AUTOMATION

Technology has completely transformed the workplace, making it possible to automate tasks, optimize processes, increase productivity, and scale operations at an extraordinary rate. But as much as technology offers opportunity, it also presents significant challenges, especially regarding values in decision-making.

Technology is not only a simple tool that always enhances our values. Often, it acts as a double-edged sword—either strengthening value-driven decisions or quietly eroding them.

In this chapter, we will explore how technology can either help or get in the way of making choices that are based on values. We will pay special attention to the role of automation in this process.

From chatbots and algorithm-driven marketing to AI-enhanced supply chains, automation offers convenience, efficiency, and cost savings. But while it's easy to get caught up in the potential of automation, there's a deeper, more complex factor to think about. It is about the role of values. As powerful as automation is, its real impact is ultimately determined by the values that govern it or the innate lack of such values.

Thus, we're going to explore why values are essential in automation and why simply "leaving it to the machine" is not enough. We'll also look at how values shape the decisions behind automation, the ethics embedded (or ignored) in algorithms, and the risks of automating without a moral compass.

Technology as an Amplifier of Values

At its best, technology amplifies our values, bringing greater clarity and impact to our actions.

For example, data analytics can help us make more ethical decisions by providing the insights we need to understand complex systems. Organizations that focus on protecting the environment use information to keep an eye on pollution and tackle the effects of climate change. Similarly, healthcare providers use patient information to develop care plans that are more personalized and compassionate.

These applications show that technology can act as a partner in our pursuit of good, enabling us to work smarter and with greater intention. In this context, technology supports and strengthens our values, enabling us to act with precision.

An AI tool that analyzes environmental impact data to help a business reduce its carbon footprint aligns a business more closely with its environmental values. Technology, in this case, solves a problem while also fostering alignment with the company's highest goals.

However, while technology can amplify values, it doesn't automatically align with them.

As automation grows, so does our responsibility to ensure it reflects the principles we hold, not just the efficiencies we seek. When values aren't central to our technology use, we risk relying on its efficiency without considering its ethical implications.

The Challenge of Dehumanization

Automation, despite its advantages, can create a sense of detachment. The further we remove human decision-making from processes, the easier it is to lose sight of the human impact. When we rely on automation, it can simplify complicated problems into just numbers or lists of tasks. This process can take away the understanding and care that people naturally provide when they are involved.

This issue is especially evident in customer service, where automated systems might respond to customer inquiries without nuance or empathy. If a business becomes overly dependent on automation, it risks losing the very personal touch that customers appreciate.

An example involves Virgin Money, whose AI-powered chatbot mistakenly reprimanded a customer for using the word "virgin" when inquiring about merging two Individual Savings Accounts (ISAs) with the company. The chatbot responded: "Please don't use words like that. I won't be able to continue our chat if you use this language," suggesting that it deemed the word "virgin" inappropriate. This incident highlighted the challenges of deploying AI tools for customer service and underscored the potential pitfalls of rolling out external artificial intelligence tools.

Such negative interactions can erode customer loyalty and lead to churn. Customers may perceive an over-reliance on chatbots as a lack of genuine care from the company, further damaging the brand's reputation.

To mitigate these risks, businesses need to ensure that their chatbots are well-designed, context-aware, and capable of handling a wide range of customer interactions without causing frustration or misunderstanding.

When automation goes unchecked or ill-designed, businesses can become distant and impersonal, favoring expedience over empathy.

This shift may seem efficient but can have a corrosive effect on brand loyalty and customer relationships. It is, therefore, important to ensure balance. When implementing automated systems, it's important to keep the human experience in focus by deliberately embedding values like empathy and responsiveness into the design.

Over-reliance on automated systems creates the risk of eroding customer trust, which is of great value for any service-based industry. Automation works best when it is guided by respect for the individuals behind the data points. We must recognize that every transaction involves real people with real emotions.

Balancing Transparency with Trust

One clear-cut way technology can have both positive and negative effects is in how we monitor and protect our privacy. While tracking data can help keep us safer, improve how things work, and give us useful information, it also raises concerns about our personal privacy. But in a world of increased digital surveillance, where is the line between transparency and invasion of privacy?

Let's look at workplace monitoring software, for example. While companies may argue that monitoring employees' work habits increases productivity, it can also create an atmosphere of distrust, where employees feel scrutinized rather than supported. This can undermine values like trust and respect, leading to resentment and disengagement.

Companies that use surveillance must do so transparently, ensuring that their technology respects employees' rights to privacy. This balance shows an approach that values both safety and privacy. It emphasizes that while it's important to feel secure, we must also respect people's right to keep their personal information private.

Automation Is More than Just a Tool

It's tempting to think of automation as a neutral force—a purely mechanical tool that does what it's told, no more and no less. But that's a misconception. Automation does what it's programmed to do, meaning it inherently reflects the values, biases, and assumptions of those who design it. Every choice we make in programming, whether we mean to or not, affects how things work. This includes every piece of code we write, the rules we create, and our decisions about which tasks to automate and which to keep done by people. Each decision we make shapes the outcomes we experience.

Consider a social media algorithm designed to increase engagement. On paper, that might sound harmless, even beneficial, as engagement is often seen as a measure of success. However, algorithms built solely around engagement metrics can prioritize sensational or divisive content, as these often generate the most interactions.

This unintended consequence shows that without a clear value framework guiding automation, we risk enabling behaviors and outcomes that, while "successful" by numbers, could damage trust, community, and even societal cohesion.

The lesson is clear: automation is only as neutral as the intentions behind it. And when it lacks a value-driven foundation, it can lead to consequences far beyond what we intended.

Ethical Questions in Automation

Automation raises ethical questions that don't always have straightforward answers. At the heart of these questions is the issue of responsibility. When a machine makes a decision, who's accountable for the outcome? Who sets the boundaries of what's ethical, safe, or fair? These are tough questions, and they underscore why values are critical in automation.

Take the example of AI in hiring. Automation can streamline resume screening, reducing hiring costs and minimizing human bias. This can be said, at least, in theory. However, without a fruitful value system embedded in the algorithm, automation can replicate and even amplify existing biases.

If past hiring data contains biases against certain groups, an algorithm trained on that data may unintentionally reinforce those biases, leading to exclusionary practices. So, who's responsible? Is it the programmer, the company, or the AI itself?

When we don't prioritize values, automation can fall into ethical gray areas, leading to results that clash with our principles. As more tasks become automated, we must ask ourselves: are we programming these systems to reflect fairness, inclusivity, and respect, or are we merely seeking efficiency?

Algorithmic Bias and the Challenge of Fairness

Another pressing issue in automated systems is the risk of algorithmic bias. Algorithms are created by humans, trained on historical data, and built within specific cultural contexts—all of which means they're vulnerable to inherited biases.

If we ignore the values embedded in our data, we risk creating systems that inadvertently perpetuate inequality.

A well-known example is predictive policing, where algorithms analyze data to identify areas with higher crime probabilities, allocating more resources to these zones. However, if the data used to train these algorithms includes biases—for example, historical over-policing in specific communities—the algorithm can end up reinforcing the same patterns. This would lead to over-policing rather than a fair distribution of resources. The values missing here are fairness and justice. Without consciously embedding them, we risk creating systems that merely amplify existing social biases.

Algorithmic bias is a reminder that automation isn't inherently fair. Without active oversight, algorithms can deepen societal divides.

Incorporating values like fairness, equality, and transparency into automated processes helps mitigate this risk, ensuring that the systems we rely on don't unintentionally harm the people they're meant to serve.

Mitigating the Risk of "Value Drift"

A major risk in an increasingly tech-driven world is the phenomenon of "value drift"—the gradual shift away from an organization's core values due to external pressures or the lure of new technologies. When businesses prioritize technology's capabilities over their own ethical principles, they can lose sight of the values that initially guided them.

One of the most striking examples of value drift in the tech space is the evolution of Facebook, now known as Meta. When it first launched, Facebook was built on the simple idea of bringing people together. It was a space where friends could reconnect, families could stay in touch, and communities could flourish. The mission was clear: to foster meaningful connections in a digital world.

But as the platform grew, so did the pressures that came with running a massive, global business. Facebook introduced the News Feed, and with it, algorithms that decided what content users saw. At first, this seemed like a way to make interactions more relevant, but over time, engagement became the driving force behind what surfaced. The more time people spent on the platform, the more ads they would see, and the more profitable the company became.

This shift wasn't necessarily sinister. It was a business adapting to its realities. But in doing so, the original intent of creating meaningful connections started to evolve. Studies later revealed that the algorithm tended to amplify sensational or polarizing content, not because anyone explicitly designed it that way, but because such content kept people engaged. The very thing that once made Facebook a place for positive connections was now fueling division in some cases, simply because outrage, controversy, and strong emotional responses were more effective at holding users' attention.

By the time internal reports began surfacing about the impact of these design choices— including concerns about misinformation and the mental health effects on young users—the company was in a different phase of its journey. Its values had not necessarily been abandoned, but they had shifted in response to the demands of scale, monetization, and competition.

Facebook's journey is a powerful lesson in how values can drift, not always as a deliberate choice, but as a result of evolving priorities. What starts as a mission-driven endeavor can be reshaped by external forces, financial incentives, and the sheer complexity of growth. It's a reminder that staying true to core values requires intentional effort.

Without it, the forces of scale, profit, and market pressures will gradually redefine what an organization stands for, sometimes in ways that those at the helm never originally intended.

To stay grounded in ethical principles while implementing automation and other technologies, we must continually reflect on our values and desired outcomes.

This will help to ensure that technological decisions align with core values rather than short-term gains. Establishing regular reviews, soliciting employee feedback, and making space for ethical discussions are some of the ways to avoid this drift and keep technology aligned with purpose-driven goals.

A New Approach to Automation

Incorporating values into automated systems takes careful planning. The key lies in value-aligned automation, an approach that ensures automation enhances, rather than erodes, the principles that define a company's identity. Instead of treating automation purely as a cost-cutting tool or simply trusting the technology to make the right choices isn't sufficient, organizations must adopt a strategy that prioritizes three key elements: human-centered design, ethical decision-making, and purpose-driven technology.

For example, organizations implementing AI in hiring could start by clearly defining what fairness means in their context. They could prioritize diversity, inclusivity, and meritocracy, programming these principles into their algorithms. By doing so, they actively mitigate bias and promote a hiring process that reflects their values. This practical approach transforms automation from a cold, indifferent process into one that genuinely aligns with the organization's ethical commitments.

Values-driven automation is about taking responsibility for how technology operates. By setting in values into our systems from the outset, we can shape technology in such a way as to make it not only effective but also conscientious.

The Cost of Ignoring Values in Automation

When values are ignored, automation can cause harm, both to people and to organizations. Scandals involving biased algorithms, public outcry over impersonal service, and even legal repercussions have all served as reminders of the pitfalls of implementing automation without adequately embedding the required values.

There are cases where companies received criticism because their hiring system seemed to prefer male applicants over female applicants. This issue raised concerns about fairness and equality in the hiring process. This wasn't an intentional bias, but it emerged because the algorithm was trained on historical hiring data from a male-dominated industry. This failure to prioritize inclusivity led to both public criticism and a tarnished reputation., If values like gender equality and fairness had been included from the start, this misstep might have been avoided.

The cost of ignoring values extends beyond financial setbacks; it also includes reputational damage.

Once trust is lost, it is hard to regain. When automation falls short of ethical standards, organizations not only risk their image but also damage relationships with customers, employees, and the broader community.

Harmonizing Values and Automation

When we instill values into automation, we ensure that as we automate, we don't lose the principles that make us human. By viewing values as an essential part of the design, we create technology that respects and supports people rather than alienates or excludes them.

Imagine a future where automation works hand-in-hand with human insight, where systems are built not only to perform but also to protect, respect, and uplift. In such a world, algorithms reflect our highest principles, from fairness and inclusivity to empathy and respect.

Do not think of it as a utopian dream. It's a reachable goal. By consciously instilling values in every layer of automation, we create a world where technology serves not only our goals but also our ethics. Automation then becomes a values-driven element that significantly contributes to our quest for a just, fair, and humane world.

Using Technology Responsibly

Technology, at its core, is neutral. It's our values that define its direction, especially when the algorithm is being designed. By aligning our tech decisions with our ethical commitments, we ensure that the double-edged sword of technology serves our goals while also staying true to our principles.

Automation guided by values has the potential to transform industries, drive innovation, and foster trust.

We must remember that each advancement in technology is an opportunity to reinforce our values, not set them aside. In every algorithm we design, every automated process we adopt, and every data-driven decision we make, we have a chance to shape the future in a way that honors our moral practices and principles by which we abide.

In the end, the question isn't whether technology is good or bad. It's how we use it. It is also whether we're willing to take responsibility for its impact. Technology offers tremendous power, but with that power comes a duty to wield it with wisdom, respect, and accountability.

10

LESSONS FROM THE FIELD

W e have explored values-driven decision-making from various angles, but the concept is only as powerful as its application. What does it really look like when values shape business choices, big and small? The personal stories of several individual professionals in various chapters of this book have largely answered this question.

In this chapter, we will explore well-known examples of organizations and leaders who have let their values guide their actions and decisions. We'll look at how these values have played a significant role in their success and the positive impact they have made, even when data alone pointed in another direction.

We'll explore the moments where values reinforced decisions, steered ethical judgment, and sometimes led to unexpected results. What would also be addressed here is how we can show that values aren't just ideals but can be powerful assets.

By the end, you'll see how values work in the field through stories that range from responsible environmental stewardship to values-driven crisis management, each revealing a facet of value-based decision-making.

These examples show that, even in a data-driven world, businesses don't have to compromise principles for progress.

Patagonia's Commitment to Environmental Stewardship

Patagonia, the outdoor apparel brand, has become a beacon for environmental values in business. For them, profit and purpose are deeply intertwined. More so, their decisions consistently reflect a commitment to environmental stewardship.

In an industry that is heavily reliant on resources, the company has chosen to limit its own growth to protect the planet. It is a bold decision that defies the common business focus on scaling and profit maximization.

An example of this is their "Don't Buy This Jacket" campaign, which encouraged customers to think twice before purchasing new items. The goal wasn't to increase sales but to promote a culture of repair, reuse, and recycling. This was something that aligned with their environmental values.

This counterintuitive approach comes with the risk of losing revenue, but it demonstrates the company's commitment to its core principles.

As a result, Patagonia did not only attract more customers but also inspired loyalty and respect from those who identified with the company's mission and ethos. Patagonia's approach shows that values can restructure traditional business practices in ways that resonate deeply with customers, adding value in ways that go beyond the bottom line.

Starbucks' Commitment to Ethical Sourcing

When Starbucks started opening stores around the world, the company promised to buy its coffee in a way that supports farmers and cares for the environment. This choice sometimes led to spending more money and facing some tough challenges, but they believed it was the right thing to do.

At the very roots of it, Starbucks is committed to building fair and respectful relationships with coffee farmers. They believe that these farmers should receive a fair payment for their work, which helps them improve their farms and adopt eco-friendly methods. This commitment is the basis of their Coffee and Farmer Equity (C.A.F.E.) Practices program, which outlines strict standards for ethically sourced coffee.

In this case, data might suggest working with cheaper suppliers to increase profit margins, but Starbucks uses a value-driven approach that considers long-term relationships, fair trade, and sustainability.

They understand that their product's quality depends on the well-being of the communities where it's grown. By choosing ethical sourcing, Starbucks isn't just protecting its brand. It's upholding a commitment to people and the planet.

Starbucks demonstrates that value-based decisions may seem costly at first but will eventually garner trust, loyalty, and a strong brand reputation. They acknowledge that this is how Starbucks can run operations laced with ethics and principles, establishing outcomes that would be invaluable in the long run.

MadeGood Granola Bars Recall (2024)

In December 2024, Riverside Natural Foods, the maker of MadeGood Granola Bars, took a bold and responsible step by voluntarily recalling over 2.4 million cases of their products. This wasn't just a minor issue but one that could have affected consumer safety. The recall was prompted by the potential presence of metal pieces in its products.

The recall was significant not just because of the sheer number of affected products but because of the swift and transparent response from Riverside. They acted quickly, acknowledging the problem and working to fix the manufacturing issue that had led to the contamination. The company assured its customers that no injuries had been reported, but they still prioritized consumer safety, opting to recall a wide range of products that spanned multiple flavors. It was a decision that could have easily resulted in a massive financial setback, as the recall affected products sold in various retail outlets across the country. Yet, Riverside's commitment to consumer safety far outweighed any concerns about profit or loss.

Despite the fact that only a small number of complaints were filed—no more than seven—according to the information available on the company's website, Riverside didn't downplay the situation. They recognized the importance of addressing any potential risk head-on. This response was a clear reflection of their values. They chose to protect their customers first, even if it meant incurring losses. It was a decision that underscored their dedication to doing what was right, rather than simply what was financially easiest.

The recall showed that no company is free from risk, but those that hold true to their values in difficult moments are the ones that earn lasting trust.

Riverside's handling of the MadeGood recall wasn't just about solving a problem; it was about affirming their commitment to the people who depend on their products. They showed that in business, as in life, values must be upheld, even when it's difficult or costly

Johnson & Johnson's Tylenol Recall

Johnson & Johnson's handling of the 1982 Tylenol crisis remains one of the most cited examples of values-driven decision-making in business. When cyanide-laced Tylenol capsules led to several deaths, Johnson & Johnson faced a pivotal choice: protect its reputation or prioritize public safety.

Rather than considering only the immediate financial repercussions, Johnson & Johnson acted quickly, pulling all Tylenol products from shelves and informing the public about the risks. The company took the situation as an opportunity to live out its credo, which emphasizes the company's duty to consumers, employees, and communities above profits.

They launched a comprehensive recall, even though it cost the company millions of dollars and required a complete overhaul of packaging standards to ensure customer safety. This decision demonstrated a deep commitment to ethical principles over profit, and the public responded positively, showing renewed trust in the brand.

By prioritizing values, Johnson & Johnson set a new standard in crisis management,

proving that businesses gain more by
protecting trust than through cutting corners.

Salesforce's Pay Equity Initiative

Salesforce, the global cloud-based software leader, made waves with a bold move that went beyond profit margins. When an internal review revealed unexplained pay disparities between male and female employees, the company did not brush it aside or bury the data. Instead, Salesforce acted decisively.

The leadership team ordered a company-wide audit and invested millions of dollars to close the gap. This was not a one-off gesture; it became an annual commitment, with resources set aside each year to ensure equal pay for equal work across gender, race, and other demographics.

From a purely financial standpoint, the initiative carried a heavy price tag. But for Salesforce, the principle of fairness and inclusivity outweighed the cost. The company framed it as a non-negotiable responsibility to its employees.

Today, Salesforce is widely recognized as a
leader in workplace equality, and its

commitment to fair pay has reinforced its
reputation as a values-driven organization.

This example illustrates that when a company makes decisions based on its core values, it can lead to positive outcomes. These outcomes include happier employees, a better reputation for the brand, and a stronger company culture overall.

IKEA's Stand Against Child Labor

As a global leader in affordable furniture, IKEA faced a major ethical challenge in the 1990s when reports emerged of child labor within its supply chains. While the company could have easily avoided responsibility, IKEA chose instead to confront the problem head-on. The company also went ahead and implemented strict policies to prevent child labor. They went further by working with UNICEF and other organizations to develop initiatives that combat the root causes of child labor in regions where it was prevalent.

This was a practical approach that wasn't about profitability. It was about aligning their operations with their ethical values of respect and social responsibility. The additional costs of monitoring and ethical sourcing were seen as investments in integrity, ultimately reinforcing IKEA's reputation as a responsible brand committed to the well-being of all stakeholders.

IKEA's response reinforces that values-based decisions often require long-term thinking, prioritizing sustainable solutions over quick gains.

Sidmach's Digital Intervention: A Stand for Youth, Safety, and Integrity

In the early 2010s, Sidmach Technologies found itself confronted not with a business pitch but a personal crisis that would lead to one of its most socially impactful innovations. The son of a company director faced significant bureaucratic hurdles while trying to register for Nigeria's mandatory National Youth Service Corps (NYSC) program. His records were inaccessible due to the NYSC's continued reliance on a fully manual system. As a result of the manual system, Nigerian graduates are required to be physically present for every transaction with the NYSC, subjecting over 300,000 young Nigerians annually to inefficiencies, unnecessary risks, and, in some tragic instances, fatal consequences.

Rather than walk away or wait for government reform, Sidmach made a bold choice: to step in and offer a technology-driven solution that would transform the entire NYSC experience. This wasn't about profit; it was a moral imperative. The company assembled a team, researched the problems extensively, and designed a comprehensive digital automation plan.

Even when government bureaucracy delayed the project, Sidmach held firm. And when tragedy struck and prospective corps members died in a bomb blast while in transit to collect physical documents, the call for change became undeniable. Shortly after, Sidmach received the green light to proceed.

Today, over 70% of NYSC operations have been automated, reducing inefficiencies, protecting lives, and restoring dignity to a rite of passage for millions of Nigerian youth.

The solution was a values-driven response to a broken system.

Google's AI Principles and Recommended Practices

In the development of artificial intelligence (AI), Google has had to weigh innovation with ethical responsibility. As one of the world's largest technology companies, they're acutely aware of the potential for AI to impact society.

With this in mind, Google established an AI ethics framework to guide its approach to machine learning and AI deployment. This includes respecting human rights, ensuring accountability, and prioritizing transparency.

Google made an important choice to steer clear of creating certain kinds of artificial intelligence that could be used for military purposes or spying. They did this because they wanted to stay true to their promise of developing technology in an ethical way. This approach may mean forgoing lucrative contracts, but it reinforces their commitment to responsible technology.

By setting ethical boundaries in AI, Google demonstrates how values can shape the future of technology.

It's a powerful reminder that the push for progress need not come at the expense of ethical considerations, even in a fast-evolving field like AI.

Ben & Jerry's Commitment to Social Justice

Ben & Jerry's has long positioned itself as a company that values social justice as much as it values creating quality ice cream.

They've used their platform to advocate for issues like climate action, racial equality, and fair-trade practices, often taking bold stances that resonate with their values.

One example is their commitment to fair-trade ingredients. Instead of sourcing the cheapest raw materials, they've invested in fair-trade cocoa, sugar, and coffee. This is their way of ensuring that suppliers in developing countries receive fair wages and sustainable conditions.

Though it could increase costs, this decision aligns with their values and has cultivated a loyal customer base that respects their commitment to positive change. Ben & Jerry's has proven that a business can stand up for important issues and make a difference. They have created a brand that represents values people believe in, which not only inspires customers but also helps keep the company strong.

Grameen Bank's Financial Inclusion Model

Grameen Bank, founded by Nobel laureate Muhammad Yunus, operates with a model that prioritizes social good over traditional profit. The bank was founded to offer microloans to the poorest populations in Bangladesh. This was with the objective of empowering individuals, particularly women so that they could start small businesses and improve their lives.

Grameen Bank's values are rooted in community development and financial inclusion, creating opportunities for economic empowerment where conventional banks saw only risks.

This approach has significantly changed the lives of many communities by helping to end poverty. It shows that when financial support is driven by strong values, it can truly make a positive difference in people's lives. Grameen Bank's approach has been replicated globally, proving that when business aligns with values like inclusivity and social responsibility, the benefits extend far beyond profit.

Grameen Bank reminds us that value-driven decisions often lead to insightful social impact, transforming lives while sustaining a thriving business model.

Lessons in Values-Driven Leadership

In business and professional life, the decisions leaders make are beyond numbers and strategies—they reflect deeper principles and values. Let's understand further from the stories of business leaders who, in their own unique ways, reveal the transformative power of values-driven leadership as well as the consequences of losing sight of these principles.

Through their journeys, we'll explore how the right values can elevate a career, shape a company's legacy, and impact entire industries. We will also learn how disregarding these principles can lead to unexpected challenges.

Ratan Tata

Tata is known for his principled approach to business. He values social responsibility and employee welfare. Throughout his tenure, he led the Tata Group with a focus on community impact, ethical sourcing, and sustainable practices.

His approach is an example of how placing values at the forefront can create lasting brand loyalty and societal impact. This proved that ethical commitments often enhance long-term organizational success and garner goodwill.

Paul Polman

As CEO of Unilever, Polman prioritized sustainability and social responsibility, driving them into the company's core strategy through the Unilever Sustainable Living Plan. By focusing on reducing environmental impact and improving community well-being, Polman showed that businesses could grow while maintaining ethical integrity.

His approach serves as a model for large corporations. It shows how they can align profit with purpose. This establishes that value-based leadership attracts both customers and investors.

Mary Barra

Barra is recognized for establishing an inclusive, ethical culture at General Motors, especially amid the company's safety recall crisis. Her emphasis on transparency and responsibility set a new tone for corporate accountability, showing that value-driven leadership is essential in building resilience and stakeholder trust.

Barra's approach shows that even during crises, prioritizing values can safeguard an organization's reputation and strengthen its ethical foundation.

Satya Nadella

Nadella transformed Microsoft's culture by cultivating empathy, collaboration, and continuous learning into the company's moral code and standard operating procedures.

His leadership style, grounded in respect and inclusivity, established an environment where employees felt empowered, leading to Microsoft's resurgence in both innovation and employee satisfaction.

Nadella's approach shows how value-driven leadership can inspire creativity, engagement, and company-wide transformation, ultimately strengthening long-term growth.

Martin Shkreli

Among other things, Shkreli became notorious for sharply increasing the price of life-saving drugs, putting profits ahead of patient access as CEO of Turing Pharmaceuticals. His approach emphasized the ethical issues of ignoring values in pursuit of short-term financial gains.

The backlash from this decision shows that focusing only on numbers can have negative consequences. It can lead to reputational damage and legal challenges. There can also be a public loss of trust. This highlights the need for value-based decision-making in business.

Elizabeth Holmes

Holmes's story epitomizes the dangers of pursuing growth metrics without ethical transparency. Driven by ambitious targets and high expectations from investors, the deceptive practices of her blood-testing company, Theranos, raised severe ethical concerns.

Holmes's downfall illustrates how a values deficit—particularly a disregard for honesty and accountability—can lead to catastrophic consequences for both the leader and stakeholders.

This accentuates the necessity of value-driven decisions in safeguarding trust and integrity.

Bernard Ebbers

Ebbers's leadership at WorldCom focused heavily on rapid financial growth, leading to one of the largest accounting frauds in history.

His decision to inflate the company's revenue demonstrated how prioritizing financial metrics at the expense of ethical standards can devastate companies, employees, and investors.

Ebbers's case serves as a cautionary tale on the perils of sidelining integrity, accountability, and transparency. It reinforces the importance of ethical structures in corporate decision-making.

BEYOND NUMBERS, VALUES MATTER

The organizations and business leaders we have reviewed reinforce that beyond numbers, values matter. Each of these examples highlights a powerful truth. When organizations and individual professionals make values fundamental to their strategies, they stand out in a competitive landscape.

In every story, we see how value-based choices strengthen not only the organization but the communities and stakeholders it touches. These examples show that while value-driven decisions may demand extra effort, they usually pay off in ways that are both tangible and deeply meaningful.

Companies and leaders that prioritize values build stronger connections with customers, employees, and communities. These choices often inspire loyalty and create a brand legacy that goes beyond profit.

As we strive to develop our businesses and careers in a world where data and efficiency play a big role, it's important to keep in mind that each of us has a personal journey when it comes to making decisions based on values. Your experiences and choices are what make your path special.

Each choice you make to prioritize values reinforces the foundation of trust and purpose that will ultimately shape the quality and extent of your influence and impact.

Conclusion

If you've reached this point, it's likely that you're already on a journey that could often be taxing. You've spent countless hours solving problems, delivering results, and chasing the metrics that define success in business. You know what it's like to meet demands, keep pace, and find validation in the outcomes of your hard work.

But even with all that dedication, perhaps you still feel a certain weight. Perhaps a sense that something essential is missing from your definition of success, that the decisions and actions you take daily need to be rooted in something more than numbers and outcomes alone.

It's not just about producing great work; it's about knowing that your work reflects your deepest principles, the ones you want to stand by in the long run.

Maybe you've asked yourself if success is really about climbing the ladder or if it's more about making a meaningful impact or even how to balance both. That uncertainty you feel is valid, and it's a signal of growth. Success isn't just about achievements or outward appearances; it's about something much more meaningful and enduring.

It comes from aligning your actions with your core values and being true to who you really are.

You've come through the chapters of this book not just to be "better" at your job but to be clearer, more certain, and more aligned with the values that make you a force for good in the world of business. You've explored the pitfalls of numbers-driven thinking and the undeniable strength that values bring to every decision.

Values like integrity, resilience, and accountability guide your growth, helping you become the kind of leader you've always aimed to be.

Imagine leading not only with skill but also with an unwavering sense of purpose. This purpose goes beyond the metrics and creates a positive ripple effect in your organization and beyond.

As you take the next steps in life, remember that every choice you make based on your beliefs is a chance to create a lasting impact. Bringing your values into your job and daily routine isn't just about being true to yourself; it's the path to creating trust, inspiring others, and achieving the kind of success that no metric alone can ever fully capture.

Let the principles and practices in this book be your foundation as you move into a world where challenges are endless, but so is your potential to rise above them. This isn't just about redefining your career—it's about living a life that you're proud of, one decision at a time.

So, take these insights and let them fuel your journey. Stand firm in your values, embrace the power of purpose-driven work, and know that your success is already unfolding.

Here's to a future where your values define your path, inspire others, and drive you to the meaningful success you've always known is possible.

INDEX

www.ingramcontent.com/pod-product-compliance
Lightning Source LLC
Chambersburg PA
CBHW040853210326
41597CB00029B/4834